THEMED DISPLAY

for early years

Story and rhyme
Displays

SHEILA DEMPSEY

THEMES ON DISPLAY for early years

AUTHOR SHEILA DEMPSEY

EDITOR SUSAN HOWARD

ASSISTANT EDITOR SAVERIA MEZZANA

SERIES DESIGNER LYNNE JOESBURY

DESIGNER SARAH ROCK

ILLUSTRATIONS JESS STOCKHAM

PHOTOGRAPHS MARTYN CHILLMAID

Enormous thanks to Cara Mead, Tracey Ludwig and all the children at Guthrie CE Infant and Nursery School, Calne, Wiltshire, who helped with all the displays.

Designed using Adobe Pagemaker

Published by Scholastic Ltd, Villiers House, Clarendon Avenue, Leamington Spa, Warwickshire CV32 5PR

Visit our website at www.scholastic.co.uk

Text © Sheila Dempsey
© 2001 Scholastic Ltd

6 7 8 9 0   6 7 8 9 0

British Library Cataloguing-in-Publication Data
A catalogue record for this book is available from the British Library.

ISBN 0-439-01813-7

Contents

Introduction   5

Chapter 1: Traditional tales   page 13
Stimulus display:
What will the story be today?   13
Interactive displays:
Oh no, you won't!   14
Plodding wins the race   16
Who's that trip-trapping over my bridge?   18
The Elves and the Shoemaker   20
Table-top display:
Sound stories   22

Chapter 2: Favourite stories   page 23
Stimulus display:
Penguins on parade   23
Interactive displays:
Elmer   24
We're Going on a Bear Hunt   26
The Rainbow Fish   28
Cuddly Dudley   30
Table-top display:
Where in the world?   32

Chapter 3: Rhyming stories   page 33
Stimulus display:
Rhyme   33
Interactive displays:
Mr McGee   34
James and the Rain   36
Ants in Your Pants   38
Over on the Farm   40
Table-top display:
Let's find out more about pigs   42

Chapter 4: Nursery rhymes   **page 43**
Stimulus display:
Favourite rhymes   43
Interactive displays:
The Grand Old Duke of York   44
Hickory, Dickory, Dock   46
Twinkle, Twinkle, Little Star   48
Sing a Song of Sixpence   50
Table-top display:
Which hat for which rhyme?   52

Chapter 5: Action rhymes   **page 53**
Stimulus display:
Making things move   53
Interactive displays:
Round and Round the Garden   54
Incy Wincy Spider   56
The Wheels on the Bus   58
An Elephant Goes Like This and That   60
Table-top display:
Come and tell a rhyme   62

Chapter 6: Counting rhymes   **page 63**
Stimulus display:
Frogs   63
Interactive displays:
Five blue boats   64
Five Little Monkeys   66
Five Little Speckled Frogs   68
Five Fat Sausages   70
Table-top display:
Working with 5   72

Photocopiable pages
Bird template   73
Dudley's shirt   74
Spinning spirals   75
Rainy days   76
Twinkle, twinkle, little stars   77
On the wing   78
One blue boat   79
Speckled frogs   80

Introduction

Creating a visually stimulating place to work and play for the youngest children in our care can be both a challenge and a thrill. An exciting, interesting and purposeful environment is essential for every child's development, in all areas of learning. This book aims to help all adults involved with working with young children to meet that challenge and to create such an environment.

Stories and rhymes provide a wealth of ideas for displays and this book can be used for whatever displays you choose to create.

When creating a display, take the time and effort to present the children's work in a stimulating way. This will help them to know that their work is valued. Most displays should contain contributions from all of the children in your setting to encourage ownership and pride in their environment. A successful display will be referred to constantly and should continue to stimulate further ideas and questioning.

Displays should provide learning and pleasure for the children and adults in the setting but should also inform parents, carers and other visitors about the current interests and topic work of the children.

Using this book

This book contains six chapters, each using a different style of story or rhyme telling – some traditional and some modern, some more and some less well-known. Despite the obvious differences in the chapters, all of the displays link closely with the requirements of the Early Learning Goals published by the Qualifications and Curriculum Authority (QCA).

Each chapter is presented in the same format. An introductory stimulus display which motivates and engages the children's interest is followed by four displays to encourage interaction. A table-top display at the end of each chapter provides further learning ideas.

Each display is divided into headings:
● Learning objective
A specific learning objective outlining the intended learning outcome is provided first.
● What you need
A suggested list of resources needed to complete the display is given. This list is intended to be flexible – substitute resources to suit your own setting and circumstances.
● What to do
This section provides step-by-step guidance for creating the effects shown in the photograph.
● Talk about
This includes ideas to encourage the children to think about the ideas behind the display, and to stimulate further discussion.
● Home links
In this section you will find useful suggestions for ways to involve the children's carers in their learning.

Introduction

THEMES ON DISPLAY
for early years

● Using the display

This section includes ideas for making the displays interactive, and ensuring that they are used by the children to the fullest.

Styles of display

The presentation of displays in your setting can take different forms. Individual paintings or drawings can be presented in a gallery style, valuing each child's work appropriately by displaying it to its best advantage. Newly discovered techniques could be displayed in a more graphic manner, perhaps displaying every child's first attempt at using pastels, for example, in a uniform style.

Making displays interactive

An interactive display should aim to encourage all children to be involved in the display content. The display should offer opportunities to answer questions set and should also pose new ones, thus stimulating enquiry. It should aim to allow the children to develop their own opinions and to foster future exploration about the content of the display and about the environment in which they find themselves.

If your display contains artefacts such as the telescope included in the 'Twinkle, twinkle, little star' display on page 48, then ensure that you take the time to teach the children how to use the equipment correctly. Add a small water tank to the 'Five blue boats'

display on page 64, to encourage lots of investigation and discussion about things that float.

If the children's work has been inspired by a particular stimulus, it is vital to include that stimulus alongside the finished display whenever possible.

Stimulus displays

Stimulus displays are intended to arouse interest, encourage discussion and elicit response from children and adults about the topic or theme that you are exploring. These displays are mainly set up by adults and should be a 'hands-on' way of encouraging the children's enthusiasm for the topic.

Remember that the most mundane objects, be they natural or man-made, can be an enormous source of interest to a child. If you intend to explore particular art or craft techniques, then make available examples or reproductions of works of art or crafts for the children to touch and examine.

Remember to include examples of the multicultural nature of our society in your displays, wherever possible.

Display tables

Display tables can be used to display children's work, books, artefacts and other resources that relate to the current displays in your setting. Provide plenty of opportunities for interactive activities on these displays. For example, in the 'Let's find out more about pigs' display on page 42, the children are

STORY AND RHYME

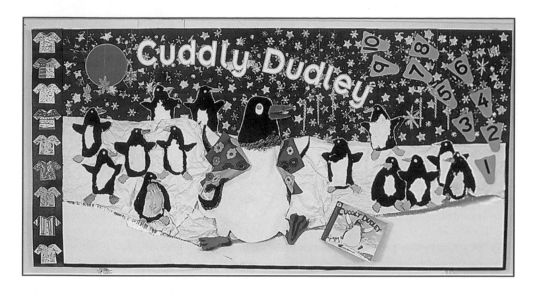

not only encouraged to find out more about a given topic but are also engaged in play.

The display table should be positioned as close as possible to the main display, allowing for transference of ideas, discussion and comparisons between the two. An interesting display table will be well accessed, and the children should be encouraged to take pride in it and to keep it tidy for others to use and enjoy.

If a low table is used for this type of display, thought should be given to creating height to the work. You can achieve this by arranging boxes of different sizes and then covering them with fabric. Make sure that this type of arrangement is secured safely to the table, especially if you are including any valuable artefacts or prized models on the table!

Constructing aesthetic displays

Help the children to develop aesthetic awareness by teaching them how to see beauty in objects and to appreciate the world around them. By constructing aesthetically pleasing displays, you will be giving them models of ways in which their own work and their environment can be enhanced to its greatest potential.

Keep up with current trends in what is considered to be 'aesthetically pleasing' by looking at the ways in which professional window and shop displays are created. Packaging, magazines and television design programmes can also provide good examples.

Throughout the year, take the opportunity to collect unusual resources that can be stored away and used at a later date. Christmas, for example, offers a good opportunity to collect shiny, glittery resources that are difficult to find at other times of the year, but that young children enjoy so much. Tinsel is perfect for a rain effect (see the 'Incy Wincy Spider' display on page 56). Wrapping paper can make a good substitute for expensive backing papers and is sometimes as good as more expensive posters.

Holidays at home and abroad, as well as visits to museums and galleries, offer opportunities to see how others approach displays and are a great chance to collect resources that are not readily available in your own local area or country. Remember that natural resources should always be left where they were found. Stress to the children

that they must never remove objects or creatures from their natural environment, and use only existing collections of sea shells. Remind them also that they must never pick leaves, flowers or fruits from trees or plants unless they have the permission of an adult. Instead, collect objects that have fallen naturally.

Curriculum opportunities

Try to represent all areas of development in your displays. Obviously some displays will be more biased to one area than others, but as you mount any display, try to question yourself as to how you could involve other curriculum areas. There is usually opportunity in most displays for captions and questions which can lead the children into thinking about different areas of learning. In most displays, there is an opportunity for number activities, for example, the number line in the 'Cuddly Dudley' display on page 30.

Displays can also be used to develop children's essential skills, which are so important in future learning. When you have completed a display, take time to discuss with the children how effective they think the display is.

Discuss labelling, what else could have been included and what parts of the display they like the best. Evaluate their answers and use their suggestions in your next display – after all, the display is there primarily for them.

Working with carers

Adults working with very small children have a great opportunity to both meet and greet parents and carers and to work with them to enhance their children's learning.

Remember to take every opportunity to inform carers about current areas of interest in your setting, and be ready to accept their ideas too. Some carers are apprehensive about what they can bring to the setting, and may need a little encouragement to share their skills or experiences with the children. But when this happens, there is benefit to all parties. The 'Home links' section for each display in this book gives suggestions for ways in which carers can take an active part in their children's learning.

Prior to setting up a new display, find a space on your notice board for a list of things that would be useful for your work. Carers are always willing to collect junk materials, and they are usually delighted to loan artefacts, photographs, treasured toys and even ornaments, providing that they know that they will be looked after properly and returned within a certain time-scale.

Consider sending home information sheets about new topics that you will be covering. This will give carers who are not able to visit the setting an opportunity to participate in their children's learning at home.

Working in 2-D and 3-D
Try to provide opportunities for all children to explore a full range of art and craft techniques in both 2-D and 3-D. Obviously this will depend on space and time restrictions in your setting, but if techniques are introduced at an early age without the barriers of knowledge, you will be surprised at the results that even the youngest children will achieve.

to the children's work and make displays visually attractive. However, remember that the display should always reflect the children's work and not be overtaken by too many sophisticated gimmicks.

Planning displays
When constructing a new display, consider the overall effect and impression that you wish to achieve before you start work with the children. This will allow for clear decisions to be made about background, sizing, positioning and borders.

Plan where your finished display will be mounted. This will help you to

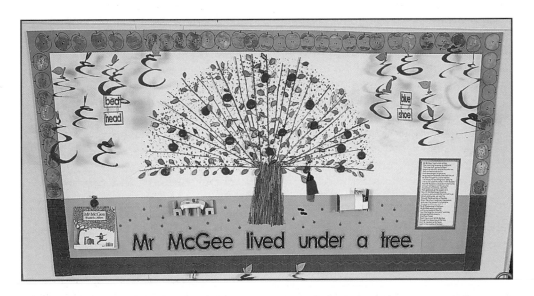

Mr McGee lived under a tree.

Working two-dimensionally, the children will be able to explore materials. This discovery work can make an excellent background for a new display, such as the 'Five blue boats' display on page 64. Encourage individual modelling work using clay, salt dough and play dough, but first, be prepared to work on rolling, cutting and mark-making, until the children are a bit more adventurous and are able to build upwards.

Work co-operatively to attempt larger pieces of work such as the papier mâché sausages for the 'Five fat sausages' display on page 70, and capitalize on the children's enjoyment of 'junk modelling' to make the 'Hickory, dickory, dock' display on page 46.

Techniques such as bending, folding, padding and using structures to support work will add 3-D interest

decide on the type and style of work that will be most appropriate for the display (2-D, 3-D or a mixture of both). Know your space. Measure your display boards or your wall spaces and make a small pencil mark on the top and side centre points of these areas. This will help you to make sure that your finished displays are level and that the work planned will fit and still look visually effective. Try not to cram too much work onto any display, or it will look muddled and confusing.

Consider displaying examples of the same work alongside the main display, or hanging work mounted back to back to increase your display space. Think about viewing points. Remember, the view of a child will be very different from that of an adult and if the display is interactive, the children need to have access to it.

STORY AND RHYME

THEMES ON DISPLAY for early years

If your setting allows, think about putting up some discrete means of hanging display facilities such as an old-fashioned pulley clothes line, or a wooden curtain rod. This will give you instant extra space on which to display the children's finished work, or for work in progress.

Safety must always be an important consideration when putting up displays. A safety ladder or kick stool will help you to reach higher or less accessible areas, but remember, whatever goes up has to come down!

Mounting and framing

Before you mount work to display, think carefully about the purpose of the mount. Backgrounds and mounts should enhance, not overpower the work. Borders that are too wide or fussy will overshadow the work, and if they are too narrow they lose their point.

Mounts can become the frames for the children's work, or the frame can be a separate addition. However, you should consider whether anything is to be gained from overpowering a piece of work with too much production.

Borders on large displays may be included to neaten edges, to complement the display or even to involve another activity in the display.

Cutting and fixing

If you have made decisions about the final display, then you can cut paper to size before the activity begins. This will give you an opportunity to encourage the children to work within their own boundaries. You may find for example that a child varies his figure drawings to denote importance, scale or size, and to then cut that paper down may detract from the child's depiction of the subject. However, if you do decide to cut paintings and still require a uniform style of display, then you could consider varying the sizes of mounts or frames.

There are a variety of adhesives available that can be used to fix work. Glue sticks are useful if the children are helping you to mount work. PVA glue is good but can cause some papers to wrinkle. Rubber latex glue is quick and flat drying and of course sticky tape, adhesive squares and putty also have their place. To fix work to walls or boards, use round-headed map pins or staples, which are unobtrusive and can be easily removed.

Semi-permanent and moveable displays

Sometimes there is no choice about how space is allotted for display. Some display spaces are just too high for the

Elmer was not elephant colour
Elmer was yellow, orange, red, pink,
purple, blue, green, black, and white.

10

children to appreciate but may offer the opportunity to set up a display for parents or visitors. Consider a plan of work for the week or the month surrounded with photographs or pictures of children busy in those pursuits, or perhaps a 'Look what we've been doing' semi-permanent display.

In settings where furniture has to be moved or packed away at the end of each session, hinged boards will allow for 2-D displays to be easily erected and dismantled.

Drapes and dividers

The use of drapes to hang alongside displays is a personal preference. In some instances, they can look too ornate and fussy, but well-chosen drapes can enhance a display. They are a wonderful device for transforming units and tables into display surfaces, or for dividing an area to make it more intimate for role-play.

Try to collect a selection of drapes in two-metre lengths. New fabrics, especially themed pieces, are expensive, so consider collecting old curtains, duvet covers, bed sheets, offcuts and even shower curtains (the transparent ones make an excellent front or backdrop for underwater displays). Be adventurous, and try using a selection of colours and textures to create different effects.

Lighting

Light can be used to create many stunning display effects. Windows offer a sometimes neglected display space. Use sticky-backed plastic to cut out words, numbers or pictures to use this space to its full potential. Windows also offer a perfect background for stained glass, and other paint effects.

Artificial light can produce interesting shadow effects that can be used for the setting of more dramatic displays, or dispelled by introducing another light source. A choice of lighter coloured backing paper will help to lighten a display, and impressive effects can be achieved using the many reflective and special effect foil papers that are now widely available.

When mounting displays in window areas, remember that strong sunlight can fade some papers and can affect some adhesives.

Labelling

When considering which labelling to use in a display about stories and rhymes, be guided by the effect you wish to create and by the wording style of the book that you are using. Some excellent lettering and templates of various fonts are now available on computer. Encourage the children to look at the captions on a display and help them to

begin to understand that the same letters can be represented in many different fonts.

The labelling on your displays should reinforce early vocabulary, inform, question and instruct.

Photographs

A camera would be beneficial in any early years setting. Activities and achievements are sometimes so fleeting that only a photograph can record these events. Seize the opportunity to record involvement, effort and achievement by displaying photographs alongside your displays. The reward will be a greater interest in finished displays, not only from the children but also from carers and visitors to your setting.

Photographs should be collected in an on-going album, to inform new and present parents, and to have as evidence for inspection.

Books and artefacts

A good selection of well-maintained books is important for all early years groups. There should be books which the children can access freely, as well as collections of books for reading at story times.

Both fiction and non-fiction books should be available to help with specific topic displays. Consider making collections of books by favourite authors, themes or styles – for example, pop-up books. This will help both adults and children to look at books with a fresh eye and make hitherto unmade connections. Books are expensive, but there are factory sales, book clubs and libraries that can also be used as sources.

Be broad-minded about artefacts. Collect and store unusual objects if you can – the time will come when you really could use that old garden gnome or

discarded bicycle wheel! A newsletter is also a great way of involving carers in your quest for interesting topic artefact or simply keeping them informed.

Display toolbox

When the children's work is completed, take a few moments to reflect on the original intentions of the display. Collect all of your 'ingredients' together including the work, backing papers and border as well as the artefacts, books, models and resources that will make the complete interactive display. Then collect your display toolbox and enjoy making a new and inspiring display for everybody in your setting!

Useful resources

Most of the resources that you will need to use to create the displays in this book will be readily available in most early years settings, but it is helpful to have a few pieces of special equipment in your display toolbox. These include:
● string/fishing line
● ruler/tape measure
● map pins
● guillotine strimmer
● craft knife
● scissors (large and small, including pinking shears)
● double-sided adhesive pads
● adhesive putty
● wide variety of coloured papers, including foil and Cellophane
● hole punch.

Traditional tales

What will the story be today?

Learning objective: to encourage conversation and discussion about story content.

What you need

Fabric; backing paper; border; card; a copy of each of the stories that you intend to explore; artefacts relating to your chosen stories; Blu-Tack.

What to do

Cover a display board with backing paper and add a bright border. In the centre of the board, attach the heading 'What will the story be today?'. Hang a copy of each of the stories that you intend to explore underneath the heading. Mount the titles of the stories on card and attach to the display. Make a second set of titles and put aside. Over the next few days, allow time for the children to discover the books during reading times and independent work time.

Place a table below the display board and cover it with fabric. Before the session, decide on the story you want to explore more deeply with the children and place the relevant artefacts on the table. For example, if you choose 'The Little Red Hen', you might include flour, ears of corn and butter. Your artefacts could relate to the whole story or to just one incident in the tale, depending on how aware the children are of the chosen text. Make a free-standing card saying 'All these things will help us to tell the story of' and ask the children to Blu-Tack the correct title of the chosen story on the card. This will help to encourage letter and word recognition.

Talk about
● During reading time, talk about how and when the artefacts on the table are used in the story.
● Encourage the children to suggest other artefacts that could be used.
● Talk about the possibility of these events happening in real life. For example, could a chicken really bake a loaf of bread? Could a gingerman really jump out of the oven?

Home links
● Encourage the children to find other versions of the same tales and ask them to bring them to your setting to compare and contrast.
● Play games at home that involve thinking of clues, like *I Spy* and *Hunt the Thimble*.

Well-loved tales are the inspiration for the colourful displays in this chapter. Re-visit old favourites such as 'The Little Red Hen' and 'The Three Billy Goats Gruff' and have some fun creating these original displays.

Oh no, you won't!

Learning objective: to use a traditional tale to communicate meaning and to explore familiar words.

What you need
Wallpaper; border paper; painting paper; blue, white, red, yellow, gold, pink and brown paint; feather-patterned paper (photocopied); red, yellow, white and black card; silver foil; variety of pink collage papers; yellow and orange paper; wool and thread; an old bucket; craft knife (adult use); newspapers; PVA glue; ears of wheat; fabric; a collection of soft toys or puppets; a copy of 'The Little Red Hen' (Traditional) and *Chick* by Angela Royston (*See How They Grow* series, Dorling Kindersley); cardboard boxes.

What to do
Read the story of 'The Little Red Hen' with the children. In some versions of

the story, the hen makes bread but in others she makes a cake. Let the children decide which version to portray.

Decide on a colour scheme for your display – we chose blue. Cover the top half of the board with wallpaper. Cut a large piece of painting paper for the table-cloth. To create an illusion of depth, mark out two lines of regular squares at the bottom, and a central vanishing point at the top. Cut out the squares, marking their order numbers on the back. Use white tonal shades to paint the even squares and blue tonal shades to paint the odd squares. When dry, piece the table-cloth together and mount on the display.

Let the children help to make the animals. Cut out a large outline of a hen. Using a photocopied feather-patterned sheet, let the children paint lots of feathers in reds, yellows and gold. When dry, cut out the feathers and glue them onto the outline. Cut features from coloured card and attach to the outline.

Using the display
Personal, social and emotional development
● During circle time, talk about helping each other, sharing and being kind and thoughtful.

Communication, language and literacy
● Read other stories about chickens, such as *Rosie's Walk* by Pat Hutchins (Puffin Books) or *Dora's Eggs* by Julie Sykes (Magi Publications).
● Find other books that use speech bubbles to tell a story, such as *This is the Bear and the Picnic Lunch* by Sarah Hayes (Walker Books).

Mathematical development
● Introduce opportunities for children to talk about sharing and early fraction terminology. What fraction of the cake would each animal have if they divided it equally?

● Use paper discs and folding and cutting techniques to explore how sharing works.

Knowledge and understanding of the world
● Make a simple map route using small world equipment to show the hen's route in the story.
● Grind some wheat to find the flour inside the grains.

Creative development
● Encourage small groups of children to use masks or puppets to retell the story of 'The Little Red Hen' to their friends. Extend the activity by suggesting different scenarios. For example, would the hen have shared the cake if the animals had helped her with just one of her tasks? How do you think the other animals felt when the hen decided not to share the cake with them?

Cover a large outline of a pig with a variety of pink collage papers. Make the nose stand out by mounting it on thick card. Cover a large outline of a cat with bands of yellow and orange paper in a stripy pattern. Add black card whiskers. To make the dog, use PVA glue to stick on wool and thread. Make the ears separately for a 3-D effect.

To make the cake, an adult should use a craft knife to slice the bottom off an old plastic bucket at a slight angle. Cut out a triangular segment to make the piece of cake for the little red hen. Cover the cake shape with PVA and strips of newspaper, adding balls of paper for decorations. When dry, let the children paint the cake with a mixture of paint and PVA to make it look shiny and delicious! Make a simple knife shape from black card and cover the blade with silver foil. Attach to the display together with some ears of wheat. Add a speech bubble for each character with dialogue from the story.

Below the display, arrange soft toys, story-books and information books on coloured fabric draped over cardboard boxes. Let the children make collaged masks in the same way as they made the figures. Make a set of sequencing cards for the children to put in order as they tell the story.

Talk about
● With the children, discuss speech bubbles in books and comics.
● Talk about the repetition of words and phrases in the story.
● Discuss the things that the hen did to turn the wheat into bread.

Home links
● Suggest that the children do some baking at home and try to find out more about ingredients and how they are processed.
● Encourage a visit to a farm or wildlife park so that the children gain an understanding of real animals and their habitats.

Plodding wins the race

Learning objective: to develop an understanding of the need for persistence and determination.

What you need

Pale blue backing paper; green and blue border paper; stiff card; brown parcel paper; green and brown art papers; brown, green, copper and orange paint; white card; print blocks; real vegetables; dowelling; pipe-cleaners; tissue paper; wire; salt dough; PVA glue; mapping pins; red clay; small toy hare (or outline); soft toy tortoises; green fabric; *Aesop's Fables* retold by Anne Gatti (Pavilion Books).

What to do

Read the story of 'The Determined Tortoise' to the children. Suggest that they help to create a display of the story, involving the use of many different creative techniques.

Cover the top part of the board with pale blue backing paper for the sky, and add a big yellow sun. Segment the rest of the board into fields using brown and green art papers. Try crumpling, folding and tearing techniques to create different textures for these areas. Add a brown parcel paper pathway, widening it at the bottom of the display to give an illusion of depth. Complete the background with a blue border at the top and a green border at the bottom.

Introduce the children to the different vegetables. You might like to do some

observational drawing, senses work or perhaps make some soup.

Once the children have explored the vegetables, encourage them to fill the fields on the display with 'creative' vegetables. Mould salt-dough carrots and attach leaves with wire before baking the dough in the oven. Paint with a mixture of paint and PVA glue. Use mapping pins to fix the carrots onto one of the brown fields. Using real cabbage leaves and green paint, print leaves onto green paper. When dry, let the children cut them out and attach them to the display in bunches to make realistic-looking cabbages.

Use print blocks to make lettuces, again attaching them in bunches. To make leeks, mark pieces of paper with green lines and roll into tubes. Attach small pieces of cut green paper to the tops of the tubes with tape, then mount them in another field. Use stiff card to label the vegetables.

Place a small toy hare, or an outline of a hare, on the far horizon. Make a winning post from white card and two pieces of dowelling for the foreground. Cut a tortoise shape from stiff card and let the children add coiled pipe-cleaners to make shell patterns and to section off the head, tail and feet. Cover the tortoise with PVA glue and a single layer of tissue paper. When dry, paint the tortoise, then secure it to the display at the winning post.

Involve the children in rolling, joining and patterning activities to make tortoise models using red clay. If you do not have a kiln, wait until the models

are completely dry before painting them and varnishing them with PVA glue.

Talk about
● Whenever the chance arises, talk with the children about the need to finish a job when they have started it.
● Talk about how important it is to really try your best, even if you are finding things difficult.

Home links
● Tell carers what you have been doing. Perhaps they could introduce their children to some other vegetable tastes at home.

Using the display
Personal, social and emotional development
● Encourage ways to reward people if they really try their best and keep on going until the end of a task.
● Invite the children to think about people whose jobs involve helping others to achieve, such as teachers or nurses.

Communication, language and literacy
● Explore other Aesop's Fables and discuss the morals.
● Discuss the meaning of 'opposite'. Help the children to make a list of opposites, such as fast/slow, hot/cold and so on.

Mathematical development
● Do some work with time using a minute sand timer. Set a simple task and see how many times the children can complete it in one minute. Make the task more challenging and set the timer again. Discuss the scores with the children.
● Make a grid on a large piece of card. Play a game using a dice and the children's clay models. Do not set the rules, this is a challenge that you can leave to the children.

Physical development
● During movement time, explore different ways to move, fast/slow, forwards/backwards and so on.

Creative development
● Use a computer with the 'Dazzle' program (SEMERC) to make pictures of decorative tortoises. Depending on the children's abilities, they may access a variety of functions to colour their tortoises.

Who's that trip-trapping over my bridge?

Learning objectives: to develop an understanding of right and wrong; to respond creatively to a traditional tale.

What you need
White, blue, brown and green backing and art paper; blue foil; brown, green, black, white and red paint; collage materials; junk cardboard boxes; sand; rope; balsa wood; wool; craft knife (adult use); marbling equipment; newspapers; PVA glue; old bucket; rubber gloves; old plastic pudding basin; card; scissors; yellow, blue and green fabric; wooden building blocks; small-world goats; a troll; a copy of 'The Three Billy Goats Gruff' (Traditional).

What to do
Read the story of 'The Three Billy Goats Gruff' together. Suggest that you build a 3-D display of the story.

Begin by making the troll's nose and hands using papier mâché. Tear five newspapers into small pieces and put them into an old bucket. Add enough water to soak the paper and leave overnight. The following day, pour off any excess water then add about a quarter of a litre of PVA glue. Mix the paper and glue until it begins to resemble thick porridge. The ink will

hands and face. Add features and woollen hair, then secure the troll to the display. Add a title, and a few extra questions.

Beneath the display, arrange fabric to represent a river. A collection of wooden blocks will encourage the children to build bridges for the goats to cross and a troll puppet will encourage role-play.

come off the newspaper, so it is advisable to wear rubber gloves. For the nose, model the mixture over an old plastic pudding basin, and for the hands cut out two large card hand shapes and model the papier-mâché over these. Leave to dry for at least three days before painting.

Cover the top of the board with blue paper to represent sky. Make the dry, stony land on the left-hand side of the river using a variety of brown paper and painted strips. Make the lush grass on the right-hand side in a similar way, using green and yellow materials. For the river, let the children experiment with marbling techniques, then add these to blue backing paper. To give the river a directional flow, add strips of dark blue paper or foil.

Invite the children to use black and white paint to paint cardboard boxes for the bridge. Let them mix the colours to give a stony effect. When dry, attach the boxes to the display to form the pillars of the bridge. Suspend a piece of rope between the pillars. An adult should use a craft knife to cut small pieces of balsa wood, and then stick the wood over the top of the rope.

Cut a goat shape out and encourage the children to use textural collage materials to cover it. Attach the goat to the display to make it look as if it is standing on the bridge.

Draw around a child to make the troll shape, enlarging the head. Encourage the children to practise their fine brush control on small squares of paper for the shirt pattern. Paint the trouser leg, adding sand to the paint for texture. Paint a boot for the troll, giving it a shiny effect by adding PVA glue to the paint. Use skin tones to paint the nose,

Talk about
● With the children, talk about the understanding of right and wrong. Who makes the rules at your setting? What happens if rules are broken?
● Carefully introduce an understanding of bullying. Discuss what can be done to help both the bullied and the bully.

Home links
● Inform carers of your discussion about bullying and encourage them to talk carefully with their children about this topic.
● Find more versions of this traditional tale and read them with the children.

Using the display
Communication, language and literacy
● Make a collection of books that rely on questions and answers to tell the story, such as *Mr Gumpy's Outing* by John Burningham (Puffin Books).
● Think of more words to describe the noises that footsteps make on different surfaces.

Mathematical development
● Work on sets of three using stories such as 'Goldilocks and the Three Bears' and 'The Three Little Pigs'.
● Introduce the vocabulary 'small', 'medium' and 'large' related to the animals in the stories.

Knowledge and understanding of the world
● Discuss what makes some land fertile and some infertile. What is needed to make plants grow well?
● Plant grass seeds in seed trays. Let the children enjoy cutting it with scissors and using it for small-world play.

Physical development
● During both outdoor and indoor play, use ropes laid on the ground for the children to balance along. When they are proficient at this, introduce low beams. Remember to give safety rules before the children use the apparatus.
● Play stepping-stone games as another way to cross the river.

The Elves and the Shoemaker

Learning objectives: to encourage working together with a friend; to learn about helping others.

What you need

Brown backing paper; cream border; shoe catalogues; wood-effect paper; card; cardboard tubes; black fine liners; painting paper; white paper; paints; collage materials; large hole punch; foil paper; spools of thread and buttons; tape measure; tissue paper; PVA glue; shoes and boots; shoeboxes; shoe rack; foot measurer; table; cash till; telephone; pad and pencil; mirror; 'The Elves and the Shoemaker' (Traditional).

What to do

Read the story of 'The Elves and the Shoemaker' and look at the pictures with the children. Can they suggest how the workbench and tools might have looked to the elves? Invite them to help you make a display showing the equipment that the shoemaker used.

Cover the display board with brown backing paper and add a cream border. Allow the children plenty of time to browse through shoe catalogues, then help them to cut out pictures of different types of footwear. Stick these around the border.

Invite the children to investigate the boots and shoes. Encourage them to make observational drawings of their chosen piece of footwear using black fine liners on white paper. Select six drawings and make A3 photocopies of them. Mount the original drawings across the bottom of the display.

Use wood-effect paper to make the shoemaker's workbench. Cut the outlines of a large pair of scissors and a needle from card, and cover them with foil paper. Cut two pieces of card into boot shapes and let the children cover them with tissue to represent leather pieces, ready to be sewn into shoes. Use a large hole punch to perforate the shapes around the edges. Add other shoe-making equipment, such as a tape measure, spools of thread and buttons. Word process or write by hand useful words such as 'leather', 'scissors', 'thread', 'needle' and 'buttons', and add them to the display.

Take the A3 copies of the children's drawings and cut them into sections. In pairs, allow the children free choice of collage and paint effects to decorate the pieces. Ensure that you mark the pieces to prevent them from getting muddled or reversed! When the pieces are dry, invite the children to help you to reassemble them. Their sense of achievement at fitting them back together correctly will help them to understand how the elves felt. Display the footwear along the sides of the workbench, using cardboard tubes for support and to give a 3-D effect. Add appropriate captions from the story.

Below the board, set up a role-play area as a shoe shop. Provide plenty of different footwear to encourage discussion and general interaction. Display the footwear on a shoe rack to encourage sorting and matching activities. Provide shoeboxes for the same purpose. Add a mirror and a foot measurer, and arrange a counter with cash till, telephone pad and paper. Add inviting signs and questions to the display to encourage an interest in reading and to help direct the role-play.

Talk about
● During circle time, invite the children to discuss people who help others both in the home and at work, such as parents, siblings, police officers, doctors, firefighters and so on.

Using the display
Personal, social and emotional development
● Discuss helping others when they are having trouble or feeling sad.
● Talk with the children about the things that they need to remember when they are working with a friend, such as sharing and taking turns, listening to each other and making joint decisions.

Mathematical development
● Work with sets of two. Use the shoe collection or pairs of socks to match, compare and count.
● Measure the children's feet and make a bar graph.

Knowledge and understanding of the world
● Find out about shoes worn in different countries and throughout the centuries.
● Make a collection of footwear worn for different sports, for example, rollerblades, ballet and tap-dancing shoes, flippers and so on.
● Make simple sandals by cutting out a sole shape from card and attaching straps (these can be both inventive and decorative).

Physical development
● During physical play, invite the children to make large movements to mimic sewing actions. Construct routes with tunnels, hurdles and tubes for the children to experience going in, through and out again.
● Give the children strips of card, a hole punch, laces and threads and encourage them to experiment with early sewing techniques.

● Talk about what everyone can do to help the people that are close to them.

Home links
● Encourage carers to make the most of their next shoe shop visit with their children. Can they compare and contrast their real experience with the role-play area in your setting? Can they suggest any additions to the role-play area to make it even more realistic?

Sound stories

Learning objectives: to respond to traditional tales using simple musical instruments; to sequence a story using appropriate story picture cards.

What you need

A low table covered with an attractive drape; four pieces of A5 card; cardholder (if possible); a copy of a traditional tale, such as 'The Three Billy Goats Gruff' (Traditional); a selection of untuned instruments which the children can play with independently; appropriate questions to lead the activity such as 'Can you make a sound story using these instruments?'.

What to do

Using the pieces of A5 card, make a set of four very simple sequencing cards which tell the traditional tale that the children want to work on. A cardholder will help to display the sequence. When the children are familiar with the story sequence, introduce a selection of untuned instruments.

Give the children plenty of time to experiment with the instruments and then encourage them to choose an instrument to fit each card in the sequence. Reassure the children by stressing that there are no right or wrong decisions. Appropriate questions and directions such as 'Can you make a sound story?' and 'Use these cards to help you to order your story' will help to lead the activity.

Talk about
● Listen to story tapes with the children and encourage them to discuss the instruments or sound effects that have been used to help to tell the story in an interesting way.
● Talk about words and about how some repetitive phrases such as 'trip-trap, trip-trap', are almost musical.

Home links
● Explain to carers what you have been doing in music time. Suggest that they help the children to look for safe things around the home that might help them to tell a bedtime story together. A wooden spoon and a baking tin make an excellent drum, and some buttons in a plastic screw-top bottle would make a perfect rattle.

Further display table ideas
● Use any of the stories featured in this chapter to build up sound stories for similar display tables.
● Make a matching game with sports footwear and pictures of sportsmen and women wearing it.

Favourite stories

This chapter provides a wide range of lively interactive display ideas based on the children's favourites, including the classic Elmer stories by David McKee, and Michael Rosen's ever-popular 'We're Going On a Bear Hunt'.

Penguins on parade

Learning objectives: to promote interest in story characters; to encourage comparative and descriptive language.

What you need
White fabric; blue painting paper; silver border paper; scraps of white paper; circle and snowflake templates; silver foil; white foam offcuts; toy penguins; information books such as *Penguins* by René Mettler (Moonlight Publishing); story-books such as *Please Be Quiet!* by Mary Murphy (Mammoth) and *Penguin Pete and Little Tim* by Marcus Pfister (North-South Books).

What to do
Cut discs and snowflakes from white paper using templates, or draw them free-hand. Stick these randomly onto blue painting paper to look like snow. Secure the background to the display board and add a silver border. Fix white fabric down the side of the display board and over the table below. Scrunch up some silver foil and make an icy pool on the table, then add a pile of white foam offcuts to look like blocks of ice.

The display board can hold a suitable caption, pictures or photographs of penguins and an information book about penguins. On the table, display the toy penguins, together with story-books that feature penguins as characters.

Talk about
● Take time to discuss the characters in the stories that you read. Talk about where the animals live, what they eat and how big they are in real life.
● Encourage the children to use comparative and descriptive language to discuss the penguins in your collection.

Home links
● Encourage a visit to a zoo or wildlife park where the children can see real animals and discover more about them.
● Ask the children to look at home for books, pictures or toys that they could add to the collection.

Elmer

Learning objective: to use the illustrations from the Elmer stories to explore colour and shape.

What you need

Yellow and green backing paper; large sheets of painting paper; yellow card; grey card; scraps of coloured card; paints; crayons; felt-tipped pens; large and small brushes; coloured sugar paper; scissors; grid paper; gold paper scraps; gold spray paint (adult use); gold foil; thin wire; PVA glue; hole reinforcers; coloured hobby foam; patchwork quilt or drape; collection of *Elmer* books and toys, including the original book, *Elmer: The Story of a Patchwork Elephant* by David McKee (Red Fox); the 'Bird template' photocopiable sheet on page 73.

What to do

Read the story of *Elmer* to the children, taking time to look at the illustrations in the book. Show the children a patchwork quilt or drape to give them an understanding of exactly what patchwork is and how it is made. Suggest that they might like to help make an *Elmer* display using some of the ideas from David McKee's story.

Cover the top of the display with yellow and the bottom with green backing paper. Cut out a large yellow card disc to make the sun. Position the sun temporarily on the backing paper and spray gold paint around the edge. The spray should take only moments to dry. Turn the card over and let the children decorate it with scraps of yellow paper and gold foil. When dry, secure the sun inside the gold spray paint circle.

Cut a large Elmer shape and a separate ear shape from painting paper. Give the children squares of painting paper cut to size, and encourage them first to decide upon their favourite colour, and then to paint their square with that colour. When the squares are dry, let the children decide where to stick them on the Elmer outline. Challenge them by asking them to make sure that no two squares of the same colour are positioned next to each other! Join the ear so that it flaps out slightly, then secure Elmer onto the display. Ask the children

Elmer was not elephant colour
Elmer was yellow, orange, red, pink,
purple, blue, green, black, and white.

Elmer was patchwork.

STORY AND RHYME

to colour and paint pieces of grid paper to make a border for the display. This will encourage concentration and perseverance as well as the use of fine motor skills with fine brushes, crayons and felt-tipped pens.

Look at the imaginative trees in the book. Let the children decide what colour tree and leaves they would like to make, and which design to use, and then provide coloured sugar paper and card for their designs. Consider using tonal colours so as not to detract from the primary and secondary colours in the Elmer painting.

Look at the illustrations of the birds in the book. Provide copies of the photocopiable sheet on page 73, or let the children use their imaginations to draw their own birds on coloured card, and then use their cutting skills to cut around their outlines. Use fine gauge coloured wire to make the birds' legs, and stick on hole reinforcers for eyes. When complete, let the children decide where to place the birds on the display. Suspend some from the ceiling if possible. Make captions for the display using colour and pattern to reinforce the desired objectives.

Place a low surface in front of your display and cover it with a patchwork quilt or drape. Draw a picture of Elmer onto grey cardboard and divide it into 5cm squares. Cut 5cm squares of coloured hobby foam to produce a decision-making activity for the children to explore. Arrange a large selection of Elmer books, puzzles and toys on the display surface.

Talk about
● Discuss the use of colour in the Elmer story. Talk about how different colours are used to suggest mood, interest and even time of day.
● Talk about the appearance of the creatures and plants in the story. Extend the discussion to explore the concept of camouflage and warning colours.

Home links
● Encourage carers to talk about crafts with their children. If you are fortunate enough to have a carer who does patchwork, knitting, crocheting or embroidering, invite them to demonstrate their skill to the children.

Using the display
Personal, social and emotional development
● Talk about what makes people different in appearance, gender and age, and about how it feels when you are different. Be sensitive to individual circumstances.
● Talk about what makes you laugh and the difference between feeling happy and sad.

Communication, language and literacy
● During drama time, challenge the children to be Elmer and to act out the story through his eyes.
● Read other books about patchwork, such as The Patchwork Quilt by Valerie Flournoy (Puffin Books) and Peter's Patchwork Dream by Willemien Min (Barefoot Books).

Mathematical development
● Work with squares and cubes to discover and compare properties, pattern and tessellation.

Creative development
● Look at books about the technique of patchwork, such as The Creative Quilter: Techniques and Projects by Pauline Brown (Guild of Master Craftsman Publications). Encourage the children to select their favourite patterns, make templates and develop the patchwork theme.

We're Going on a Bear Hunt

Learning objectives: to encourage the growth of imaginative vocabulary; to explore sound and texture.

What you need

Painting paper; green and yellow paper; scissors; pipe-cleaners; red beads; paints in a variety of colours; cardboard combs; clay; wellington boots; PVA glue; twigs; white foam; sand; silver glitter; cardboard offcuts; thin black border; brown fabric; collection of found objects or instruments to make sound effects such as plastic and metal kitchen utensils and dried pulses; *We're Going on a Bear Hunt* by Michael Rosen, illustrated by Helen Oxenbury (Walker Books).

What to do

Read the story with the children looking carefully at the illustrations and discussing the sound words used to describe the different events. Challenge the children to think about how they could represent each part of the story sequence using art and craft materials.

Divide the display board into six sections. Cut painting paper to the required size for each section and work on one section at a time in the correct sequence. Mount the display as each section is completed, as this will help the children to remember the order of the events in the story when re-telling.

Begin by cutting 'long wavy grass' from green and yellow paper to stick onto the first section. Add simple flowers made from pipe-cleaners and red beads.

To represent the 'deep cold river', ask the children to use blue, green and white paint, and cardboard combs to make wavy water.

Brush brown paint roughly onto the next section to make 'thick oozy mud'. Make some footprints for the mud. Roll clay to a thickness of about 2cm and ask the children to put on their wellington boots before stepping onto it. Carefully cut around the footprints. When dry, gloss them with PVA glue and then secure onto the display.

For the 'big dark forest', invite the children to make a rough, textured base using dark green and brown paint. Attach real twigs to make the forest floor.

To make the 'whirling swirling snowstorm', encourage the children to paint freely with white and grey paint. When this is dry, liberally add small pieces of white foam and silver glitter.

The final part of the sequence is the 'narrow gloomy cave'. Paint a simple seaside background and let the children glue on sand for the beach. Use cardboard offcuts to build a cave shape on the shore.

Use different font sizes and colours to make your captions, reflecting those used in the book. Add a narrow black border around the display.

Place a low surface in front of the display. Arrange the brown fabric on the surface and then add a collection of objects and instruments to make sound effects for the different events in the story. These could include a pan containing some rice; a sealed plastic bottle of water; a wet sponge in a bowl; plastic bricks in a bowl; shells; cones; wood shavings; coconut shells and a rainmaker.

Talk about
● With the children, discuss how the author uses words to give atmosphere to the story. Notice how the words are printed in different sizes to make the storytelling more exciting.
● Talk about the illustrations, observing how some are black and white and some colour. Can the children work out how the illustrator made the pictures? What tools did she use?

Home links
● Tell carers that you have been looking at this particular story. Encourage them to look in their cupboards and garages to find more sound effects which might help to tell the story!

Using the display
Personal, social and emotional development
● Although we do not know the characters' names, a lot can be learned about them by studying the illustrations. Who are the carers and who is being cared for? Does this change during the story? Which characters are most afraid of events and when? Study the dog throughout the story and see how his character develops!

Communication, language and literacy
● Find other stories that rely on sequences, such as *The Shopping Basket* by John Burningham (Red Fox).
● Make a list of more sound words that describe places or events. For example, think of sounds to describe Bonfire Night, such as 'pop' and 'bang'.

Mathematical development
● Use the sequence of the story to talk about ordering. What happened first, second, third, last?
● Use the events in the story to encourage the children to practise counting on and counting back.

Knowledge and understanding of the world
● Talk about the possibility of the events happening in one short walk out with the family.
● Invite the children to help you make a simple map of the story, and use it as the basis for a board game.

Creative development
● Ask the children to choose a character from the story. Retell the story, adding reminders about events such as holding up skirts, taking off shoes and running up stairs. Encourage a small group of children to use the sound effects to help their friends act out the story.

STORY AND RHYME

THEMES ON DISPLAY
for early years

The Rainbow Fish

Learning objectives: to use a variety of art and craft techniques; to encourage sensitivity to the needs and feelings of others.

What you need

A copy of *The Rainbow Fish* by Marcus Pfister (North-South Books); lining paper; blue and green Brusho (available from Specialist Crafts, tel: 0116-2510405); large and small paintbrushes; pale green border paper; green and white painting paper; blue card; paints; coloured and clear Cellophane; orange and yellow papers; foil paper; green pipe-cleaners; coloured beads; PVA glue; plastic bottles and pots; newspapers; kitchen paper; rainbow wrapping paper; rainbow fabric; collection of underwater toys and puppets; small-world sea creatures; collection of shells, net, driftwood and so on. (**NB** Use only existing collections and remind the children that they must not remove any objects from beaches.)

What to do

Read the story of *The Rainbow Fish* to the children. When you have finished, read it through again, this time paying close attention to the illustrations. Ask the children if they have any ideas about how they could make one of their favourite pictures in the book into a display.

Roll out lengths of lining paper the same height as the display board. Ask the children to put on aprons and let them paint the paper using water and large household paintbrushes. When the paper is wet, sprinkle on Brusho powder. This produces a stunning

watery effect and creates a wide range of tones when the colours mingle. When the paper is dry, cut it into strips of different widths and use these for the background to the display. Add a green foreground to represent the sea-bed, and a pale green border.

Cut out a large Rainbow Fish and choose a palette of colours, taking guidance from the illustrations in the book. Invite groups of children to paint the head, tail and fins. When these sections are dry, let the children sponge them again using a different colour. Cut individual scales and let the children paint them with the colours from your chosen palette. Cover some of the scales in silver foil.

Invite a group of children to stick the finished scales onto the fish outline, starting at the tail and overlapping until they reach the head. Cut the little fish from blue card and let a group of children use blue collage materials to decorate it. Attach to the board, facing the Rainbow Fish. Secure a silver foil scale to the Rainbow Fish's fin.

Arrange strips of coloured Cellophane and green pipe-cleaners threaded with beads on the background to add to the underwater atmosphere. Attach clear Cellophane discs above the fishes' mouths to represent bubbles.

Cut crab and starfish shapes, and encourage the children to cover them with collage materials. Finish with a coat of PVA glue. Fold the creatures before stapling to the display, to give a 3-D

effect. Add a caption cut from rainbow wrapping paper.

To make the hanging fish, help the children to stick plastic pots to the ends of plastic bottles to make the base models. When they are happy with the shapes, help them to cover their models with strips of newspaper and PVA glue. Finally, cover each fish with a layer of glue and kitchen paper. When the models are dry, paint and decorate them and add coloured Cellophane for fins and tails. Suspend from the ceiling in front of the display.

Place a low surface in front of the display and cover it with rainbow fabric. Display a collection of underwater soft toys and puppets, small-world sea creatures and seaside objects.

Talk about
● Talk about the different techniques that you used to make the display. Which was the children's favourite activity? Why?
● Talk about the different characters in the story and about how they might feel when the Rainbow Fish decides to give them a shiny scale.

Home links
● Encourage carers to talk to their children about making and staying friends with other children.

Using the display
Personal, social and emotional development
● Talk with the children about how they can be kind to others and how they can help children who are not yet happy to be away from home.

Communication, language and literacy
● Read other stories that deal with the issue of keeping friends such as *The Lazy Bear* by Brian Wildsmith (Oxford University Press).

Mathematical development
● Make a fish sorting game. Use different-coloured felt to make the stuffed fish, and give the fish different-coloured gills and eyes to encourage sorting for different criteria.
● Sort your shell collection by type, size or weight.

Knowledge and understanding of the world
● Use information books such as *Seashore* by Steve Parker (*Eyewitness* series, Dorling Kindersley) to find out about underwater life.

Creative development
● Make underwater creatures using clay. Use modelling tools to press in different patterns.

Cuddly Dudley

*Learning objectives: to respond to a
favourite story using a variety of paint
techniques; to encourage creative
design; to encourage number skill
development.*

What you need

A copy of *Cuddly Dudley* by Jez
Alborough (Walker Books); black
and white painting paper; white,
green and orange drawing paper;
white corrugated paper; silver foil;
orange and black card; paints; silver
glitter glue; print blocks; number
templates; large piece of white fabric;
large dice; children's flippers; the
'Dudley's shirt' photocopiable sheet
on page 74.

What to do

Enjoy the story of *Cuddly Dudley* with
the children. Invite them to help you
make a display about the story using
ideas from the illustrations in the book.

Lay some large pieces of black
painting paper on a table and prepare
some printing blocks of snowflakes and
stars. These can be ready-made or
handmade using potato halves.
Throughout the session, invite groups of
children to randomly print snowflakes or
stars onto the paper to make the
background for your display. Add some
sparkle by drawing little stars with
glitter glue. Secure the printed sheets to
the display board.

To make the snowy landscape,
crumple up sheets of white drawing
paper, then smooth them out and staple

Using the display

Personal, social and emotional development

● Explain that everybody needs time to be by themselves sometimes. During circle time, ask the children what they like or dislike about being by themselves. What do they do with that special time?

Communication, language and literacy

● Look at a collection of non-fiction books to find out more about the different species of penguin, the penguin's life cycle and its habitat. (See the stimulus display in this chapter.)

Mathematical development

● Encourage the children to play the penguin footprint game with a friend, taking turns to wear the flippers and throw the dice. This will help them to develop number skills and co-operative play.

Knowledge and understanding of the world

● Use the small-world plastic penguins and other polar animals in the water tray. Add blocks of white sponge to represent icebergs, and provide real ice cubes – it will make the activity even more exciting!

● Discover more about ice. How long does it take to make ice from tap water? How long does it take for the ice to melt back to water? Why does ice melt? Why do we freeze food?

Physical development

● Devise an obstacle route outside. Use chalked footprints or arrows for the children to follow.

them below the starry sky. The foreground is made with two pieces of ripped, white corrugated paper backed with a fine edge of silver foil. Place a large orange moon in the sky.

Give the children plenty of opportunity to look at toys and pictures of penguins. Explain that, although all the penguins in the display will need to be roughly the same height, with black and white bodies and yellow beaks and feet, the children can also make their penguins unique!

Provide white paper and encourage the children to draw their penguins to fit the paper. During one session, invite the children to paint the black areas of their penguins. During the following session, ask them to paint the white and yellow areas. Mount the finished penguins onto silver foil and cut them out with a 5mm border.

Cut out a large outline of Cuddly Dudley and invite a group of children to paint him. Add silver glitter to white paint to make Dudley's tummy sparkle. Cut green drawing paper to size to make the front of Dudley's shirt, and encourage the children to colour it with bright flowers.

Provide each child with a copy of the shirt template on page 74 and invite them to design a shirt for Dudley using a range of colours and patterns. Display the shirts along one side of the board, attaching a black border to the other three sides.

Arrange some white fabric in front of the display. Draw around a child's flipper onto orange card to make ten 'penguin footprints'. Number these from one to ten to make a dice game for the children to play. Smaller numbered footprints can be placed onto the main display to add another interactive opportunity.

Talk about

● Talk about the characters in the story and especially about how Cuddly Dudley had so many brothers and sisters and needed time and space to be on his own.

Home links

● Tell carers about the number games that the children are playing with the penguin footprints. They might like to make a similar game at home, perhaps using wellington boots instead of flippers.

● Encourage carers to watch wildlife television programmes with their children. This will help the children to gain an understanding of the lives of real animals, as well as those in story-books.

THEMES ON DISPLAY for early years

Where in the world?

Learning objective: to discover more about animals in stories, especially where they live.

What you need
Blue fabric; large map of the world; globe; small-world animals, birds and sea life; information books such as *Animals* (*First Facts* series, Kingfisher Books) and *Birds* by Jill Bailey (*Eyewitness Explorers* series, Dorling Kindersley); an atlas such as *My First Atlas* by Bill Boyle (Dorling Kindersley).

What to do
Cover a large table with blue fabric and lay a large map of the world over it. Place various small-world animals, birds and sea life on the map along with a collection of information books, an atlas and a globe. As the children will probably need to be taught the differences between the globe, the map and the atlas, introduce them gradually in order that there is some understanding that all three resources represent the same thing.

Gradually introduce a range of information books for the children to look at and to help to answer their questions about animals, birds and fish, or those set by adults or friends. Label the table map with the names of some countries to encourage early reading and memory skills.

Talk about
● Talk about how to use the map, atlas and globe.
● Discuss the differences between climates in various parts of the world and how animals have adapted to living in those conditions.
● Talk about how we decide what clothes to wear according to the season.

Home links
● Encourage carers to find pictures or holiday photographs of different parts of the world to show to their children. This will help them to gain an understanding of the world.

Further display table ideas
● Invite the children to choose a country that they would like to know more about and to select books and resources about that country.
● Make a collection of clothes, some for a beach holiday and some for a skiing holiday. Divide a table into two halves, and hang a cut-out sun over one half. Over the other, stick some snowflakes on the wall. Encourage the children to sort the clothes onto the appropriate sides of the table.

Rhyming stories

Rhyme

Learning objectives: to begin to associate objects and their sounds with patterns in rhyme using a favourite story; to encourage listening skills.

What you need
White paper; border paper; coloured card; coloured fabric; *Ants in Your Pants* by Sue Heap (Scholastic); collection of rhyming objects; two word cards for each object; table.

What to do
Cover a display board with white paper, and add a border. Hang coloured fabric down the side of the display board and over the table below. On the board, display a copy of *Ants in Your Pants*, together with sets of rhyming words such as 'pig' and 'wig', 'snake' and 'cake'. Mount these word pairs onto coloured card, to give children who are not yet able to recognize whole words a clue for matching. On the table, place a collection of objects to sort into rhyming pairs, such as a small plastic pig and a play wig, and some plastic ants and a pair of pants. Have another set of word cards available so that the children can label the objects correctly.

Talk about
● Talk about what 'rhyming' means, what it is used for and where we find it. Discuss how rhyming words are used in poems and songs as well as in stories.
● Talk to the children about how they can help you to make similar collections of objects for each of the other stories in this chapter.

Home links
● Tell carers about the current theme of work in the setting. Suggest that they visit the library with their children to look for more rhyming stories.
● Suggest that carers emphasize rhyming words when singing songs or reading rhymes with their children.
● Play games that involve listening, such as *Simon Says* and sound lotto (for example, *Soundtracks*, available from Living and Learning, tel: 01223-864894).

Get into the rhythm of some fun rhyming stories to create these stunning displays. Ideas include a Mr McGee display to stimulate language and role-play skills, and a number display based on the counting rhyme 'Ants in Your Pants'.

Mr McGee

Learning objectives: to encourage children to role-play a favourite rhyming story; to develop an awareness of rhyme.

What you need

A copy of *Mr McGee* by Pamela Allen (Puffin Books); white and green backing paper; green painting paper; paint; green border; red and green paper; the 'Spinning spirals' photocopiable sheet on page 75; scissors; large hole punch; brown cardboard; reeds or sticks; salt dough; wire; PVA glue; dolls' house furniture; small pieces of coloured felt; apples; green fabric; role-play clothes; collection of apple peelers and corers.

What to do

Read *Mr McGee* to the children. On the first reading, concentrate on the story line, but during subsequent readings, spend some time looking at the rhyming words and the illustrations. Try to reflect the clear and simple style of illustrations in your display.

Make some salt dough with the children. Over two sessions, make apples and leaves for Mr McGee's tree. Before baking the salt dough in the oven, stick a 5cm piece of wire into each item. When the leaves and apples have been baked and cooled, let the children paint them with a mixture of paint and PVA glue.

Lay a large piece of white backing paper on the floor and mask out a

semicircle for the top of the tree. Invite a group of children to dip their fingertips into green paint and print the background leaves for the tree. When dry, staple into place on the display board. Attach green paper to represent grass at the bottom of the display.

Cut some reeds or straight sticks to the correct size for the branches of the tree. The children can help to wind the wired salt-dough leaves and apples onto the sticks to make the branches. Secure the branches to the finger-painted area of the display, using staples or pins. Cut a piece of brown cardboard to make the trunk and ask a group of children to glue on the remaining reeds or sticks. When dry, secure the trunk in place. Let the children use red paper and a large hole punch to make some apples which have fallen from the tree.

Invite groups of children to print the top border of the display using real apple halves dipped in paint. Outline the prints when dry, and let the children use felt-tipped pens to add pips and cores. Add a green border to the bottom of the display. In the story, Mr McGee peels and eats the wiggly skin of an apple that has fallen from the tree. Copy the photocopiable sheet on page 75 onto red paper and encourage the children to cut their own spiral apple peels. Attach the leaves and cores to the top of each spiral, then hang the apples over the display. Make some rhyming word cards such as 'cat' and 'hat', and 'head' and bed', to hang in between the spiral apples.

Add small-world furniture to complete the display, together with some clothes for Mr McGee, cut from felt, hanging from a low branch of the tree. Add a caption. A complete version of the rhyme mounted on the wall will encourage carers and children to interact with the display.

Below the display, place a table and cover it with some green fabric. Lay a collection of apple peelers and corers and add some clothes like those worn by Mr McGee, to encourage discussion and role-play.

Talk about
● With the children, talk about the rhyming words in the story and about the rhythm of the rhyme.
● Talk about the possibility of this story really happening and about some of the differences between fact and fantasy.

Home links
● If a carer who lives close to the setting has an apple tree in their garden, perhaps they will allow your group to visit. The story would certainly come to life if you could read it to the children in the shade of a real apple tree.

Using the display
Communication, language and literacy
● Make illustrated lists of words that rhyme, and hang them near to the display.
● Discuss Mr McGee's feelings throughout the story, such as surprise, glee and fear.

Mathematical development
● Develop early understanding of fractions as you complete the apple print border.
● Use opportunities for positional language development as you talk with the children about the display and the story.

Knowledge and understanding of the world
● Use small-world equipment to make a picture map of Mr McGee's journey.
● Make a picture book with the children about a year in the life of an apple tree from bud to fruit.

Creative development
● Use musical instruments to tap out the rhythm of the rhyme in the story.
● Encourage the children to collect and make prints of different leaves to compare their shapes and colours.

THEMES ON DISPLAY for early years

James and the Rain

Learning objectives: to stimulate discussion about the rain, umbrellas and rainwear; to explore tonal colour mixing.

What you need

Painting paper; fine black border; silver lametta (stranded foil Christmas tree decoration); card; paint; shallow tray; paintbrushes; sponges; selection of yellow and gold shiny papers; bamboo cane; wellington boots; umbrellas; yellow and black fabric; *James and the Rain* by Karla Kuskin, illustrated by Reg Cartwright (Hodder); the 'Rainy days' photocopiable sheet on page 76.

What to do

Enjoy this beautiful rhyming number story with the children. The illustrations hold a wealth of interesting talking points from rain and rainwear, to animals and number activities. Talk about the style of illustration and discuss how the children could help to create their display using a similar style.

Invite the children to experiment with mixing black and white paint. Let them discover whether it is best, to make grey, to start with white and to add black, or to start with black and then to add white. Challenge the children to see how many different greys they can mix. Cut some strips of painting paper the width of the display board and ask groups of children to paint them using different grey tones. When dry, scallop one edge of each strip and mount them, overlapping, to cover the top two thirds of the board.

Do some similar work using green and black paint to cover the bottom third of the board. Stick thin strips of grey and silver paper and some silver lametta over the grey sky to make the rain. Cut two large cloud shapes from card and ask a group of children to paint and sponge them to look like stormy clouds. Suspend over the display. Make some weather word labels such as 'storm', 'drizzle' and 'shower', and suspend these from the clouds.

Cut out a large figure of James from card. Invite a group of children to cover his coat and hat with a selection of yellow and gold shiny papers, then ask individual children to add details to the coat and to paint the face, hands and boots. Attach James to the display.

Cut out a large umbrella shape from card. Cut it into sections and let the children paint it using the grey tonal collection that they created for the sky. When dry, reassemble and secure in place above James. A bamboo cane works well as the umbrella handle.

Add a title to your display, and include a verse from the rhyme as a stimulus for discussion.

Let the children have some fun making footprints. Encourage them to put on their wellington boots and step into shallow trays of paint and then onto paper to make prints of different colours. When the prints are dry, cut

them out and place them with the wellington boots in front of the display. Add a collection of different-sized and different-coloured umbrellas.

Talk about
● Talk about dressing up to go out in the rain. What are the differences between the clothes and footwear that we wear on rainy days and those we wear on dry days?

● Encourage the children to talk about the umbrella collection. Compare sizes and handle shapes. What materials are the umbrellas made from? Are they all intended to be used in the rain?

Home links
● Invite carers to go for a walk with their children on a rainy day. The children will love the puddles and watching the rain coming out of a drainpipe.

Using the display
Mathematical development
● Use small-world animals to role-play the number themes in the story.
● Play matching and sizing games with the wellington boot collection.

Knowledge and understanding of the world
● Make a collection of different materials such as cotton, plastic and nylon. Devise experiments to find out which materials are waterproof.
● When the rain has stopped and the sun has come out, take small groups of children outside and use chalk to draw around the puddles. Revisit the puddles later or the next day and see if they have begun to disappear. Where has the water gone?

Physical development
● Take an imaginary walk in the rain. The children can pretend to dress up for the rain, put up umbrellas and go jumping in puddles!
● Encourage the children to develop their fine motor control by joining the dots and colouring the photocopiable sheet on page 76.

Creative development
● Collect shade cards from a DIY store and invite the children to each make a tonal strip from white through to black.
● Use musical instruments to recreate the sounds of the rain and splashing in puddles.
● Sing some rainy songs and rhymes together, such as 'I Hear Thunder', 'Incy Wincy Spider', 'Doctor Foster' and 'Rain, Rain, Go Away'.

Ants in Your Pants

Learning objectives: to create patterns; to discover more about shapes and their properties; to gain awareness of language in number.

What you need

Orange backing paper; orange, green, black and white drawing paper; fine black border; green, black and white painting paper; paint; paintbrushes; scissors; PVA glue; cardboard; newspapers; sticky tape; kitchen paper; paint; square print block; black and white gingham; black fabric; threading beads; pattern cards; toy snakes; *Ants in Your Pants* by Sue Heap (Scholastic).

What to do

Read the story *Ants in Your Pants*. The children will enjoy the funny rhyming words and the amusing illustrations.

Most children have a fascination for snakes, a love of cakes and a growing interest in numbers – and this display combines all three!

Tell the children that you are going to make a display of patterns. Ask them to choose four main colours – we chose black, white, green and orange. Cover the display board with orange backing paper. Cut out some small snakes and encourage the children to work on patterns using fine paintbrushes and the chosen colour palette.

Cut out seven snakes, four from green painting paper (for the odd-numbered snakes) and three from black painting paper (for the even-numbered snakes). To add an extra dimension to the display, make the snakes into the shapes of the numbers. Invite the children to decorate the snakes in order, using coloured paper cut into different shapes for each number. For example, discs for snake

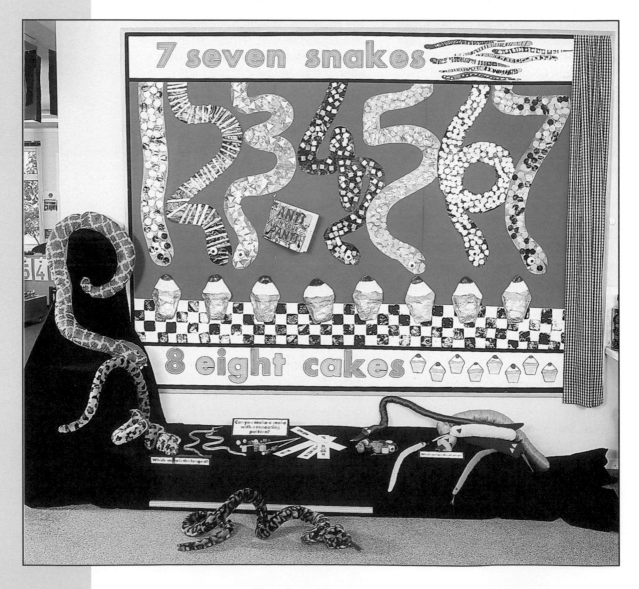

number one; a two-stripe pattern for snake number two and so on. Give each snake a beady eye before adding to the display. Add a caption at the top of the board, and display the children's small patterned snakes alongside.

Create the bottom section of the display. With a group of children, look at the black and white gingham fabric, then challenge them to use a square print block to print a chequered cloth. Encourage another group of children to paint some small cut-out cakes. Attach these along the bottom of the display, with a caption.

Cut eight cake shapes from strong cardboard. Invite the children to screw up pieces of newspaper and stick them onto the cakes with sticky tape. When the cakes are well padded, cover them with a couple of layers of newspaper and PVA glue. Add a final layer of kitchen paper to give a good painting surface. Leave to dry for a day or two, then ask the children to paint them, using just two colours for the cake cases. Arrange these on the display in an alternating pattern. Add a fine black border to frame the display and separate the captions from the main picture.

Arrange black fabric over a low surface beneath the display. On this, arrange beads, rods, laces and pattern cards for the children to make their own bead snakes, a snake dice game and a collection of small-world and toy snakes for the children to play with and to compare for length and pattern.

Talk about
● When the display is complete, talk about all its elements – the rhyme, the numbers, the shapes and the patterns.
● Talk about why the snake's faces change from smiles to frowns on the next page of the story.

Home links
● Perhaps you have a carer who keeps snakes and who might be willing to visit your setting to show them to the children. If you can arrange a visit, you

Using the display
Personal, social and emotional development
● Take time to talk about being the odd one out. Discuss what it feels like to be left out and how to deal with those feelings.
● Set up some role-play or drama situations that involve the children in sharing bricks, pencils or sweets.

Communication, language and literacy
● With the children, recite or sing other rhymes that involve numbers such as, 'One, Two, Three, Four, Five, Once I Caught a Fish Alive',
● Ask the children to help you make lists of other words that rhyme with numbers, such as – one, bun, sun; two, shoe, blue; three, sea, tree.

Mathematical development
● Go for a pattern hunt and look for patterns on floors, on buildings, in gardens, and on the street.
● Play matching pairs with the children. Socks, shoes and gloves are good resources that are always available for these games.
● Play with a selection of mosaic shapes. Talk about the properties of the shapes and introduce the concept of tessellation.

Knowledge and understanding of the world
● Look for more patterns in nature, for example, zebras, tigers, giraffes and Dalmatians.
● Use two sets of natural objects to make patterns in the sand.

can be assured of not only a memorable session but also an opportunity to allay some fears, and a chance to find out more about these fascinating creatures. Remember to follow your setting's policy on inviting animals onto the premises.

Over on the farm in a warm muddy pen...

...lived a kind mother pig and her little piggies ten!

Over on the Farm

Learning objectives: to listen attentively to a rhyming story, predicting what comes next; to talk about animals and their young; to discuss memories of babyhood.

What you need
Dark backing paper; pink border paper; white and pink painting paper; pink collage papers; scissors; PVA glue; red, crimson, white, yellow, ochre and brown paint; acetate or Cellophane; art straws; paintbrushes; plastic goggly eyes; brown fabric; farm layout with animals and their young; puzzles of animals and their young; *Over on the Farm* by Christopher Gunson (Picture Corgi).

What to do
Enjoy the story of *Over on the Farm* with the children. Look at the picture of the kind mother pig with her little piggies ten. Invite the children to think about how they could help to make a display like the picture.

Cover a display board with dark backing paper and add a pink border. Ask groups of children to cut small pieces of pink collage papers to stick onto large sheets of pink painting paper. When the sheets are dry, cut out a large pig shape and staple it to the centre of the display. Cut out two ears and give them a dark pink border before folding them and stapling them into position. Add other features such as a snout, eyes and a curly tail.

Let the children use yellow, ochre and brown to paint some art straws. When these are dry, attach them to the board together with strips of acetate or Cellophane to make a bed of straw for the piglets.

Encourage the children to look at the illustration of the pig family again, this time looking carefully at the piglets. Each piglet has a different character. Challenge the children to each paint their own piglet, independently, over two sessions. During the first session, they should paint their pigs disregarding fine details or features. Provide red, crimson and white paint, and encourage the children to mix them together to make the desired colours. Remind them that they must make their piglet look different from their neighbour's! When the piglets are dry, cut them out.

During the second session, invite the children to mix a darker pink to add ears, snouts, trotters and tails. Plastic goggly eyes will make the piglets look full of mischief! Mount the piglets on white or dark-pink paper and cut them out with a small border.

Ask the children where they would like their piglets to sit on the display. Secure them in place, adding more straw to make the pen look cosy. Add a caption circling the pig family.

Below the display, cover a low surface with brown fabric. On this, set up a farm layout and some puzzles of animals with their young.

Talk about
● Listen carefully to the rhyme in the story. Encourage the children to try to pick out the rhyming words.
● Talk about the animals in the story. Discuss the correct names of young animals, for example, piglets instead of piggies.
● Talk about how important it is to have somebody who looks after you and keeps you safe.

Home links
● Tell carers about the work that the children are doing about animals. They may be able to arrange a visit to a local children's farm to see the animals at close hand.
● Ask carers whose child has a new kitten, rabbit or hamster whether they

Using the display
Personal, social and emotional development
● During circle time, encourage the children to share their memories of their baby years. How have things changed now that they are more grown-up? What is it like when a new baby brother or sister joins the family?
● Invite the children to bring in recent pictures of themselves and some of when they were babies. Collect the pictures and make a display entitled 'Then and Now'.

Communication, language and literacy
● Make a collection of rhymes and songs about pigs or other animals from the book, such as 'This Little Pig Went to Market' and 'Five Little Ducks Went Swimming One Day'.
● Learn some of the more unusual names for the animal young such as cygnet, eaglet and cub.

Knowledge and understanding of the world
● Use the sand tray to build a farm environment for the small-world farm animals. Encourage the children to make walls or barriers to pen the animals and their young together.

Creative development
● Make piggy banks using a similar technique to that used to make the hanging fish for the 'Rainbow Fish' display on page 28.
● Encourage caring family role-play by introducing baby dolls, baby clothes and cots into the role-play area.

would like to bring it in to show their friends and to talk about animal care. Remember, always follow your setting's policy about animals on the premises.

Let's find out more about pigs

Learning objectives: to increase factual knowledge about the characters in fiction stories; to gain awareness of the difference between fiction and non-fiction.

What you need
Wooden blocks or boxes; pink fabric; small-world and soft toy pigs; pig ornaments; pig information books such as *Pigs* by Rachael Bell (Heinemann); stories about pigs such as *The Pig in the Pond* by Martin Waddell (Walker Books); pink card; pig template or computer graphic.

What to do
Arrange some small wooden blocks or boxes on a display table and cover with pink fabric. This will give height to the display and make it visually more interesting. Separate the pig books into fiction and non-fiction to encourage awareness of the different genres. Display the collection of pigs alongside the books. Invite the children to explore and add to the pig collection, and to pose and find answers to their questions by using the non-fiction books available. When you have found the answers to the questions, write the facts onto pig-shaped cards and add them to the display.

Talk about
● Talk about how pigs are portrayed in stories. Are the characteristics given to pigs in fiction stories fair?
● Talk about real pigs, and what the children have found out when using the display.

Home links
● Suggest to carers that a visit to a farm would enhance the children's awareness and understanding about farm animals.
● Encourage carers to help their children understand where common foods such as meat, eggs and milk come from.

Further display table ideas
● Similar display tables could be set up for the different animals featured in this chapter, such as snakes.
● Set up a weather chart for a month. Invite the children to fill it in every day with appropriate weather symbols. At the end of the month, tally up the symbols to see whether there have been more rainy days or more sunny days. Add a barometer and a rain gauge to the display as well as some weather pictures and information books.

Nursery rhymes

All young children love nursery rhymes, and this chapter builds on their enthusiasm by offering colourful display ideas based on favourites such as 'Hickory, Dickory, Dock' and 'Twinkle, Twinkle, Little Star'.

Favourite rhymes

Learning objectives: to promote discussion about favourite rhymes; to use technology to record rhyme-making.

What you need
Paper; card; crayons; tape recorder and microphone; colourful tin containing nursery rhyme clues (for example, a star for 'Twinkle, Twinkle, Little Star' and a toy soldier for 'The Grand Old Duke of York'); nursery rhyme books such as *This Little Puffin...* compiled by Elizabeth Matterson (Puffin Books); puzzles; nursery rhyme tapes.

What to do
Sit the children on the carpet, and discuss their favourite nursery rhymes. Decide on four of the most popular rhymes and make a 5cm square drawing for each of those rhymes. Photocopy plenty of these drawings and in the next session encourage each of the children to choose their favourite nursery rhyme picture and colour it in. When the pictures are complete, let the children help you to compile a bar graph. This can be displayed on a board with appropriate questions surrounding it such as 'Can you work out which is our favourite nursery rhyme?' and 'How many children liked "Twinkle, Twinkle, Little Star"?'.

On a table beneath the board, place a tape recorder with a microphone which the children can use to record themselves singing. Place commercially produced tapes, puzzles, poetry and nursery rhyme books on the table.

Add the colourful tin containing nursery rhyme clues. This can be used at song time to encourage the children to sing a variety of rhymes rather than just the old favourites!

Talk about
● How do you feel when you sing? Do different songs make you happy or sad?
● Invite the children to help you make up new versions of rhymes to record or to perform.

Home links
● Remind carers how important it is to sing nursery rhymes at home with their children.
● Send home the words of some of the more unusual nursery rhymes that you are learning together for the children to practise at home with their families.

The Grand Old Duke of York

Learning objectives: to think about the use of positional language; to look at large numbers.

What you need

Painting paper; paints; a range of paintbrushes; foil paper; glitter; potato print blocks; coloured border, a collection of green papers; cardboard boxes; green fabric; a collection of toy soldiers; a selection of musical instruments; the nursery rhyme 'The Grand Old Duke of York'.

What to do

Take the children outside on a fine day and look at the sky. Talk about the clouds and the colours that they can see. Working outside or inside, provide the children with large pieces of painting paper and a range of brushes to paint the sky. Let them work individually or with a friend. If the paper is white or blue, it will not be necessary to completely cover it. When the paintings are dry, staple them to the board.

Cut a simple, large castle shape from paper and invite the children to print all over it using a potato block and a mix of white and black paint to create a stone effect. Staple the castle to one side of the display and add a flag made by the children.

Tear off large pieces of green papers (drawing, painting and tissue paper), crumple them up and then smooth them out again. Arrange these to create a grassy hill shape in the bottom half of the display.

Talk about soldiers' uniforms with the children. Ask the group to decide on a uniform colour for the soldiers to wear. Decide on a jacket and trouser colour and perhaps a shape and colour for the soldiers' hats. Give the children appropriately-sized paper and invite them to paint their soldiers. They may find it easier to do this painting over a couple of days to prevent colours running into each other. When the paintings are complete, encourage the children to add buttons, stripes or

badges using shiny foil or glitter. One soldier should be decorated slightly differently from the others. He will be the Duke of York. When the soldiers are complete, staple the Duke at the top of the hill and position the others going up, coming down and at the bottom of the hill.

Print a narrow border with black arrows – some pointing up and some pointing down – and attach to the display. Finally, add an appropriate caption.

Pile some boxes on a table below the display and cover them with green fabric to make a hill. Make a 3-D castle by turning a cereal box inside out and printing it with the same potato block as was used for the large castle. Cut the top of the box to look like battlements and then reassemble the box. Place some toy soldiers in different positions on the hill to encourage the children to use positional language and a selection of musical instruments that might be played in a marching band.

Add a complete version of the rhyme to your display, together with number cards displaying the numbers 10, 100, 1,000, 10,000, 100,000 and 1,000,000.

Talk about
● Encourage discussion about larger numbers. Ask the children to think about house numbers, telephone numbers and car numbers.
● Talk about people who give us instructions, such as teachers, policemen, and doctors. Think about why it is important for everybody to follow rules and to obey instructions.

Home links
● Invite parents or grandparents to tell their children about any experiences they have of wearing a uniform and, if possible, to show it to them.
● Invite any carers who wear a uniform for their work to come in to talk about their uniform and what it is like to take or give orders.

Using the display
Personal, social and emotional development
● During movement time, arrange the children in a line. Determine who will be the Duke and put him or her at the front of the group. Tell the Duke to give, first, just a couple of instructions, such as 'stand straight', 'sit down', and then to gradually add some more and at a faster pace. The Duke could wear a special hat and the children could take turns at being the Duke. Encourage each child to talk about how it feels to be in charge.

Communication, language and literacy
● As the children become confident with the use of some positional language, gradually introduce it into games and general use.

Mathematical development
● Make a collection of larger numbers from magazines and lottery or raffle tickets. These are useful to talk about and compare.

Knowledge and understanding of the world
● Find books that feature flags from other countries. Challenge the children to design their own flags.
● Do the children know who the current Duke of York is? (Prince Andrew, the Queen's second son.)

Physical development
● Lay out some large bricks or sturdy boxes in a circuit and sing the rhyme with the children as they go up and down around the circle. Suggest that they raise and lower their arms at the appropriate positional words.

THEMES ON DISPLAY
for early years

Hickory, Dickory, Dock

Learning objective: to explore number and time in rhyme.

What you need
Nursery wallpaper; large boxes; paints; yellow, gold and black scrap papers; coloured sand; drawing paper; paper plates; black fine-line pens; mounting paper; card tubes; wool; clocks and watches; books about time such as *My First Book of Time* by Claire Llewellyn (Dorling Kindersley); bright fabric.

What to do
Sing the nursery rhyme together. Discuss why the mouse may have been running up the clock, and how the children could make a display of the rhyme.

Cover the wall space with wallpaper and add a border. Select three large cardboard boxes and let the children help to decide how they would be best arranged to make the grandfather clock. Let groups of children paint the boxes with a mixture of brown paint, sand and glue, to give texture. Encourage another group to paint and decorate lengths of card with the same mixture. When dry, use these to decorate the clock. Cut a

rectangle from the central column of the clock and attach a pendulum, made from two paper plates painted gold.

Cut a paper clock face and let the children cover it with scraps of yellow or gold paper or collage materials. Cut numbers, hands and a smile to complete the clock face.

Ask the children to draw some cats. Provide books for them to refer to, then let them use black fine-line pens for their drawings. Mount on contrasting paper and attach to the display. Enlarge two drawings to A3. Invite the artists to paint their cats and then add black sand to define the markings, and short pieces of wool around the outlines to make them look furry. Place one cat at the bottom of the clock and one at the top.

Make two mice by cutting two 15cm pieces of cardboard tube and sticking on wool and strings to make them look furry. Add whiskers, tails and ears. Make one mouse to run up the clock and the other to run down

Add a title and place clock sounds and words around the area. Arrange a collection of clocks, watches, timers and books about time on a fabric-covered surface beneath the display.

Talk about
● Talk about times that the children are familiar with, such as mealtimes, time for school, time for bed.
● Discuss events in the day that can be ordered by time.

Home links
● Ask carers to make a point of talking about time at home, looking at clocks and watches and helping to reinforce the vocabulary that you are introducing.

Using the display
Communication, language and literacy
● Collect other rhymes and stories about time such as *Bedtime Rhymes* (Ladybird Books) and *The Bad-tempered Ladybird* by Eric Carle (Puffin Books).
● Write and draw about events in the children's day. Sort this work into time order and make concertina-style books.

Mathematical development
● Let the children make paper plate clock faces. Ask them to look at the real clock collection and then to record some of the numbers on their own clocks.
● Use stop-watches to time the children doing activities, for example getting ready to go out for play. Record the result to see if they can beat their times the following day.

Knowledge and understanding of the world
● Discover how people told the time before clocks were invented, perhaps by using candles or looking at the sun.
● Open an old clock and explore the insides, looking with a magnifying glass at cogs, wheels and springs. Make drawings of what you can see.
● Use construction equipment to make clock models with moving parts.

Physical development
● Play whole-group games that involve time such as 'What's the time, Mr Wolf?'.
● Play the traditional game of 'Cat and Mouse'. Sit the children in a circle and choose a cat and a mouse. The cat has to chase the mouse around the circle and try to catch him before he gets back to his place.

Creative development
● Make a collection of wheels, springs and other mechanical objects. Roll out discs of clay and make impressions using the objects. When the discs are dry, paint them with colours similar to those found inside a real clock.
● Make a collection of musical instruments that will help the children to learn how to play a steady beat. Try counting five steady beats and then five chimes on the triangle.

Twinkle, Twinkle, Little Star

Learning objective: to enable discussion about day and night and other natural phenomena.

What you need

Blue and black backing paper; black border; black and grey painting paper; black, white, silver, gold and yellow paint; a range of paintbrushes; printed star shapes; silver spray (adult use); gold foil stars; gold card; star print block; silver foil paper for lettering; silver/gold fabric; collection of books about stars and the night sky, such as *I Wonder Why Stars Twinkle and Other Questions About Space* by Carol Stott (Kingfisher Books); toy telescope; diamond mosaic bricks; star design cards; the 'Twinkle, twinkle, little stars' photocopiable sheet on page 77.

What to do

Recite the rhyme several times with the children. Ask them which colours they think would be suitable to use for the background of this display. Cover the top half of the display board with blue and the bottom half with black backing paper. An adult should spray silver paint onto the top half. Randomly place small gold foil stars to make the night sky look spectacular.

Print a thin black border with golden stars and add it to the sky section of the display.

Talk about night-time with the children. What do their houses look like in the dark? Remind them that even though it is dark, there is light coming from the moon and the stars and so they will still see windows, doors and chimneys on their houses.

Let the children choose from a selection of dark painting papers to make a picture of a house. Provide black, white and silver paint and encourage the children to mix the colours and to paint their pictures. Some children may need to return to their paintings the following day to add details. When complete, cut the houses out and arrange them on the black area at the bottom of the display.

Give each child a copy of the photocopiable sheet on page 77. Provide yellow, white and gold paint. Encourage the children to use fine brushes to mix the colours and to paint their stars as carefully as they can. When the stars are complete, cut them out and stick a few onto the top of the display. Stick the remaining stars back to back and suspend them from the ceiling.

You can use a telescope to get a closer look at the stars.

Do you know what stars are made of?

Cut one large star from gold card. Score and fold it so that it will stand out from the display. Invite the children to cover it with lots of shiny stars, then mount it in the centre of the display, with lines of foil paper radiating from it. Add a caption from the rhyme, using letters cut from silver foil.

Cover a table or box with gold or silver fabric. Display a collection of books about stars and the night-time, including rhyme books and stories, and add a toy telescope to the display to stimulate conversation. Wooden mosaic diamonds and star-shape cards will encourage the children to design their own tessellating stars.

Talk about
● Discuss the night sky with the children. Can they describe the stars and the moon?
● Talk about the sky during the daytime. Discuss the sun and the clouds. How is the daytime sky different from the night sky?
● Discuss other natural phenomena, for example, lightning, floods, drought and so on.

Home links
● Ask carers to take their children outside when it gets dark to look at the night sky. Encourage them to make notes of their children's observations.

Using the display
Communication, language and literacy
● When the children have a clear knowledge of the rhyme, try changing the words slightly and making a new version.
● Make a list of other night-time rhymes such as 'Wee Willie Winkie', 'Golden Slumbers', and 'Hush-a-Bye Baby', and read them to the children.

Mathematical development
● Invite the children to count the stars hanging from the ceiling above the display. Make up a new song with the words 'Ten gold stars, hanging in the sky' to the tune of 'Ten Green Bottles'.
● Ask the children to count the houses in the display. Encourage them to compare shapes and sizes.

Knowledge and understanding of the world
● Use the books on the display table to find out more about stars. Why do we only see them at night? How big are they? How far away are they?

Physical development
● During physical play, encourage the children to practise making star shapes with their bodies, both standing up and lying down.
● Play a sun and moon game. When the sun is out, the stars have to hide away and be very quiet, but when the moon is out, the stars can run and jump.

Creative development
● Let small groups of children choose suitable musical instruments to accompany the other children's singing of the night-time rhyme collection.

THEMES ON DISPLAY
for early years

Sing a Song of Sixpence

Learning objective: to use a range of creative 3-D techniques to express response to a well-known rhyme.

What you need
Red and gold backing paper; black and gold border paper; junk boxes and tubes; newspapers; black and yellow card; black, gold, white and red paint; hole reinforcers; sand; Mod-Roc (available from Specialist Crafts, tel: 0116-2510405); PVA glue; foil sweet-wrappers; nylon thread; crown template; colouring materials; staple gun; the 'On the wing' photocopiable sheet on page 78; role-play clothes; play money; the rhyme 'Sing a Song of Sixpence'.

What to do
Sing the nursery rhyme with the children and discuss the different elements of the rhyme. Invite them to help you make a display showing the blackbirds flying out of the pie.

Cover the top half of the display board with gold backing paper and add musical notes cut from black card. Cover the bottom half with red paper. Give each child a crown template and encourage them to decorate it using their own choice of colours. Attach all the crowns across the bottom of the display. Add a black border around the top of the board and a gold border around the bottom. Cut discs of card and invite the children to wrap them in foil sweet-wrappers. Attach to the border to look like shiny money.

To make the blackbirds, invite the children to wrap 24 cardboard tubes (each 15cm long) with newspaper. Secure with sticky tape to make bullet-shaped bodies. Using a mixture of water

and PVA glue, encourage the children to cover the bodies with more newspaper to strengthen them.

Leave to dry for a day before painting the birds with a mixture of black paint and PVA glue to make them shiny. Once dry, use hole reinforcers to make the birds' eyes. Using the templates from the photocopiable sheet on page 78, cut wings, legs and tails from black card and beaks from yellow card. Staple these onto the painted bodies to complete the blackbirds.

To make the pie dish, cut the shape from a large cardboard box, folding side panels to form the sides of the dish. Ask a group of children to paint the dish with a mixture of white paint, sand and PVA glue. This will give a good texture and cover any blemishes on the box. When dry, mark on some stripes for the children to paint red. Attach loops of nylon thread to the back of the dish and suspend in the centre of the display.

To make the pie crust, help the children to use cardboard junk to construct the basic shapes. You will need two pieces of pie crust – one for each side of the dish. Cover the shapes with Mod- Roc, and when they are completely dry, let the children use gold paint to decorate the crust. Staple this above the pie dish.

Suspend the completed blackbirds over the pie with nylon thread. Arrange the wings of the blackbirds to make them look as if they are in flight and place a few in the opening of the pie. Display the complete version of the rhyme, and choose one line for the main caption.

Set up a clothes line near the display to hold a selection of royal clothes, and a place for the king to count his money.

Talk about
● Recite the rhyme phrase by phrase. Explain to the children what the difficult words mean.

Using the display
Personal, social and emotional development
● Discuss the different roles in the rhyme. Would the children prefer to be kings, queens or maids?

Communication, language and literacy
● When the children know the rhyme well, encourage them to pick out the rhyming words.

Mathematical development
● Hang number cards from 1 to 24 on the clothes line. Encourage the children to look for numbers that they know, or for patterns in the number line.

Knowledge and understanding of the world
● Look at books about birds and discover how to care for them.
● Collect recipe books and magazines with pictures of pies and pastry.

Creative development
● Encourage the children to use musical instruments to play a steady beat to accompany the rhyme singing.
● Re-tell the rhyme one phrase at a time and let the group re-enact the story.
● Design new crowns for the king.

● Discuss the roles of the people in the royal household. Compare them with the roles of people in families today.

Home links
● Ask parents or grandparents to talk to the children about pre-decimal money. Ask if you can borrow some (particularly a sixpence), to show to the children and to compare with present day coinage.
● Suggest that carers make pastry with their children at home. This will give the children lots to talk about during discussion time.

Nursery rhymes

THEMES ON DISPLAY
for early years

Which hat for which rhyme?

Learning objective: to encourage role-play.

What you need
Small, sturdy boxes; bright fabric; a selection of different hats belonging to characters in different nursery rhymes; card; coloured thread; felt-tipped pens; nursery rhyme books.

What to do
Using sticky tape, secure some small, sturdy boxes to your display table, and cover the arrangement with bright fabric.

Depending on the size of the table, make an initial collection of about five or six different hats that relate to well-known nursery rhymes. Make luggage style labels for each of the hats with both writing and illustrations on them. For example, you might have a mob-cap which you could label 'This hat belongs to the maid who is hanging out the clothes'. The illustration might be a washing line with clothes hanging from it.

During discussion time, encourage the children to look at and try on the hats, then show them the luggage labels. When they have decided which label

matches which hat, you can secure them with the coloured thread.

During role-play, allow the children to play freely with the hats, encouraging them to sing the appropriate nursery rhyme for the hat that they are wearing.

When the children become familiar with the hats, replace them with a new selection. This will ensure that the display remains stimulating.

Talk about
● Discuss what the characters from the different rhymes might say to each other if they met.
● Find out about people who wear hats for their jobs today.
● Talk about how styles, shapes and materials of hats have changed over the years and centuries.

Home links
● Ask carers to help their children to look through magazines for pictures of people wearing hats, to cut them out and make them into a book.

Further display table ideas
● Make a display about castles and the people that lived in them, and talk about life in medieval times.
● Create a display table entitled 'How to make a pie'. This could include a recipe, ingredients and even some tasting activities!

Action rhymes

Making things move

Learning objective: to find out why things move and how they work.

What you need
Coloured card; glue; stapler; fabric; sticky tape; split-pin fasteners; collections of toys with wheels and springs, or which spin.

What to do
Set up a display board and fabric-covered table. Place the title of the display 'Making things move' in the centre of the board. Arrange the toys on the table and invite the children to explore them. Over a few days, introduce the collections in more detail and take time with small groups of children to listen to their ideas about how the toys work. Provide card, scissors, and joining equipment and let the children experiment. As they discover different ways to manipulate the materials and the capabilities of those materials, introduce different techniques to further their skills.

Demonstrate how to use split-pin fasteners to attach moving wheels. Encourage the children to try folding, spiralling, sliding and pop-up techniques. Add the children's work to the display to encourage others to have a go.

Talk about
● Discuss how the children could use their new-found knowledge about making things move to build with construction equipment that is already in your setting.

● Talk about how things around us move. Can the children make comparisons between the things around them and their own models?

Home links
● Ask the children to look at their toys at home and to explain to their carers how they think that they work. Perhaps they could bring in other examples of toys that move to add to your display.
● Suggest that carers take their children around the home, look at some of the mechanical equipment such as bicycles, clocks and cooking utensils, and talk about what they see and how things move.

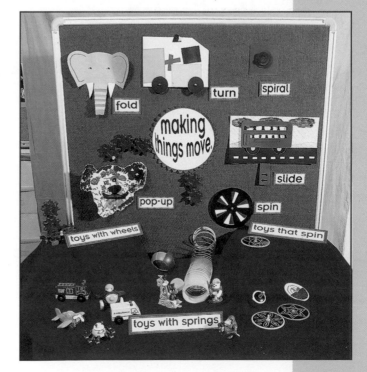

Action rhymes provide the ideal starting point for the interactive displays in this chapter. Among others, there are ideas to create an 'Incy Wincy Spider' display with a climbing spider, and a 'Round and round the garden' display with rotating teddies!

Round and Round the Garden

Learning objective: to use a range of creative techniques and design skills to make a moving display relating to a well-known rhyme.

What you need
Green backing paper; white painting paper; paints; paintbrushes; sponges; large pieces of cardboard; one large nail; hammer (adult use only); tissue paper; collage papers and materials; PVA glue; felt-tipped pens; a collection of teddy bears; a small table and chairs; role-play equipment for a picnic tea; the rhyme 'Round and Round the Garden' from *The Kingfisher Nursery Collection* (Kingfisher Books – out of print, try libraries) or *This Little Puffin...* compiled by Elizabeth Matterson (Puffin Books).

What to do
Familiarize the children with the rhyme 'Round and Round the Garden', reciting it several times. Talk with the children about how we tell the rhyme and about the movements involved. Invite them to help you make a moving display which tells the rhyme.

Introduce the bears and discuss their appearance, colour and texture. On a blank piece of paper, demonstrate how to use a stippling method with brown paint to create the texture of a teddy bear's fur. Provide paper, paints and brushes and encourage the children to paint their own bears. When the paintings are dry, return to them and show the children how to create realistic-looking eyes by cutting paper discs and adding black centres for the irises.

Cover the display board in green backing paper. Invite the children to paint tree foliage using yellow and green paint. When the paintings are dry, cut them to resemble treetops. Add trunks and branches cut from brown paper, and staple the completed trees to the background.

Depending on the size of your display board, cut three discs of strong cardboard, each with a different diameter, and make a small hole in the centre of each disc. Let the children use green collage papers and materials to cover the largest disc. Cut twelve shaped topiary trees: four discs, four squares and four triangles and ask the children to cover them with green and yellow tissue paper cut into the same shapes. When dry, paint the trunks brown. Attach the trees to the outside of the largest disc. Hammer a large nail into the board and slide the disc onto the nail so that it rotates freely.

Take the next smallest cardboard disc and invite the children to cover it with scraps of darker green paper. Attach some of the children's painted bears to the outside of this disc and place it over the largest disc. Finally, use grey collage paper to cover the smallest disc. Add the words 'Round and Round the Garden'. Place this over the nail.

To cover the head of the nail, cut a small disc from thin card and ask the children to use felt-tipped pens to colour some beautiful flowers for the centre of the garden. Attach this disc to the head of the nail using very strong glue. You should be able to spin each of the three strong cardboard discs independently.

Add the rest of the painted bears to the display, and attach some small soft toy bears. To complete the display, add the words from the rhyme.

Talk about
● Look at and discuss the finished display together.
● Spin the discs to make the teddies move 'round and round the garden'. Talk about how exciting it is to see the children's work on the move!
● Discuss how we move around. What games do the children play in their own gardens or at the park?
● Make a collection of books with moving parts or pop-up pages and encourage the children to talk about how they think the books work.

Examples include the pop-up book version of *Old Bear* by Jane Hissey (Hutchinson) and *Where, Oh Where, is Kipper's Bear?* by Mick Inkpen (Hodder).

Home links
● Suggest that carers take their children to the park for a picnic tea with their bears and maybe some of their friends.
● Make a handout sheet of finger rhymes that carers can help their children to learn and enjoy at home.

Using the display
Communication, language and literacy
● Make lists of words that describe different ways that we move, for example, quickly, slowly, happily, sadly.
● Ask questions that will encourage the children to use positional language, for example, 'Where is the bear with the longest legs?'.

Mathematical development
● Count the bears and discuss their similarities and differences.
● Talk about the shapes of the topiary trees and about the pattern that they make around the circle.

Knowledge and understanding of the world
● Find out more about real brown bears, where they live and what they eat using information books such as *Bears* by Laura Bour (*First Discovery* series, Moonlight Publishing).

Physical development
● Use chalk to make a circular route outside for the children to follow with hoops, quoits or stilts.

Creative development
● Introduce the use of split-pin fasteners and encourage the children to make their own moving models.

Incy Wincy Spider

Learning objective: to talk about weather conditions and effects using a well-known rhyme as a stimulus.

What you need

Buff backing paper; painting paper cut into brick-sized rectangles; white paper; brushes; paints; textural collage materials such as rice, lentils and sand; blue border; blue and gold foil paper; toy spider; two large cardboard tubes (both approximately 1m long, but one with a larger diameter than the other); black card; PVA glue; string; plastic tubing approximately 30cm in length; collection of toy spiders; the rhyme 'Incy Wincy Spider' found in *The Kingfisher Nursery Collection* (Kingfisher Books – out of print, try libraries) or *This Little Puffin...* compiled by Elizabeth Matterson (Puffin Books); books and games about spiders.

What to do

● Sing the rhyme 'Incy Wincy Spider' with the children and make sure that they know all the actions.

On a rainy day, take the children for a short walk outside to see how the rain runs down the drainpipes. Notice how the pipes are connected to the wall, and spend some time examining the wall itself. What do the bricks feel like? What patterns do the bricks make? Invite the children to help you make an interactive display showing Incy Wincy Spider climbing up a water spout.

Begin by covering a board with buff backing paper. Invite the children to paint the brick shapes using paint in brick colours and textural collage materials. Encourage them to experiment with the materials so that each brick is different. When the shapes are dry, let a group of children help you to use them to create a brick wall on the backing paper. Leave space within the pattern to display the rhyme.

Mix black paint with PVA glue and let the children paint the two cardboard tubes. Sew a long length of strong thread to a toy spider. Using a large needle, pass the thread through

a length of plastic tubing adding a large bead at the end to prevent it from unthreading. Secure the plastic tubing to the display board. Fix the larger cardboard tube in place over the tubing, so that the top of the cardboard tube is level with the top of the tubing. When you pull on the string, the spider should disappear up the cardboard tube. Mount the smaller tube onto the display. Add pieces of black card to represent the fixings.

Add a blue border to the display, and decorate it alternately with suns and raindrops cut from shiny foil paper.

Provide white paper and let the children use shades of blue paint to make watery patterns. When the paper is dry, cut raindrop shapes and suspend them over the top of the display. If you wish, you can include watery words on the reverse of the raindrops, such as 'splash', 'drip' and so on.

Talk about
● Talk about how the weather affects us. How do animals cope with different kinds of weather?
● Discuss how we protect ourselves against the weather by sheltering or by wearing special clothing.

Home links
● Inform carers of the work that you are doing. Suggest that they take their children out for a walk in rainy weather to look at what happens to the rain and where it goes.
● A visit to the park in the rain will allow the children to see what the ducks do when it rains.

Using the display
Personal, social and emotional development
● During circle time, invite the children to imagine that they are the spider who lives up the drainpipe. How would they feel if the rain kept on washing them out after they had spent a lot of effort climbing up? What does it feel like if people are not kind to you?

Communication, language and literacy
● Make a collection of other weather rhymes and stories. Compare them to 'Incy Wincy Spider'. Are there any similarities?
● Use play tunnels or barrels to elicit language about what it might feel like being the spider up the drainpipe.

Mathematical development
● Spiders have eight legs. Make a collection of other toy creatures which have eight legs.
● Ask questions such as 'If one spider has eight legs, how many legs will two spiders have?'.

Knowledge and understanding of the world
● Collect different fabrics and devise some experiments with the children to find out which fabrics are waterproof.
● On a sunny day, ask the children to bring their wellington boots. Put bowls of water outside and allow the children to have a paddle with their boots on. Remove the water and ask the children to walk around the area. How long does it take for the footprints to disappear in the sunshine?

The Wheels on the Bus

Learning objective: to acquire knowledge about how pop-up toys and books work and to transfer that knowledge into a working display.

What you need
Blue and black backing paper; black border paper; white sticky labels; white painting paper; coloured card; scissors; large cardboard box (about 15cm deep); six wooden spoons; two cup hooks; string; collage materials; split-pin fasteners; glitter; paints; brushes; sponge pad; PVA glue; craft knife (adult use); umbrella; toy buses; red fabric; bus timetables and artefacts; musical instruments; *This Little Puffin...* compiled by Elizabeth Matterson (Puffin Books).

What to do
Sing 'The Wheels on the Bus' (found in *This Little Puffin...*) with the children,
and invite them to suggest other verses. Look at some pop-up books and toys, and books with moving parts. Discuss the possibility of making a display that might have some moving parts.

Cover the top half of a display board with pale blue backing paper and the bottom half with black paper. Dip a sponge pad into blue paint and, using a short ruler or piece of card, print rainy lines onto the pale blue sky. Add strips of white sticky label to make road markings on the black paper. Stick smaller pieces of label along some black border paper and attach around the display.

Cut some shapes from card to make a bus stop and traffic lights. Help the children write three verses of the rhyme in the traffic light circles.

Ask the children to suggest what they might need if they were waiting for a bus in the rain. Look at an umbrella and notice that it is made up of many sections. Cut some complete umbrella shapes and divide them into triangular

sections. Invite the children to paint them with their chosen colours. Add PVA glue to the paint and a sprinkle of glitter to make the umbrellas glisten. Attach across the bottom of the display.

Make a bus from the cardboard box. Using the craft knife, cut two long window shapes and six holes at the bottom of the box for the spoon handles to slot through. Ask the children to paint the box with a mixture of red paint and PVA glue. Slide a piece of black card into the back of the bus behind the windows and glue in place. Attach two cardboard wheels using split-pin fasteners. Cut a door from red card, and either cut windows using a craft knife, or stick on strips of black paper. Add captions and numbers to complete the bus, then secure it to the display by attaching string and suspending it from two cup hooks.

With a group of six children, talk about skin colours. Provide paints in a range of skin tones and encourage the children to use the colours or mix their own to paint six wooden spoons. When these are dry, use collage materials to add features, hair and clothes. Slot the wooden spoon passengers into place in the bus. Ask another group of children to make passengers for the top deck using pieces of card cut to the same size as the spoons. Glue these into position inside the bus. Add a caption and words from the rhyme to complete your display.

Underneath the display, arrange a table or boxes covered with red fabric. Display toy buses and bus artefacts and make a board for tickets and timetables. Include a selection of musical instruments for the children to use as accompaniment when they sing the song.

Talk about
● Discuss bus journeys. How do they vary from journeys by other forms of transport?
● Where might the children travel to on a bus?
● Talk about what you can see when you are sitting upstairs on a bus.

Home links
● Suggest that, for a special treat, carers take their children on a bus ride.

Using the display
Personal, social and emotional development
● During circle time, talk about different skin colours. This can be a sensitive subject, so it should be managed with care.

Communication, language and literacy
● Arrange for a real bus driver to come and talk to the children. Before the driver arrives, make a list of questions that the children can ask. Record the questions and answers and, afterwards, make an illustrated book about what you found out.
● Make a collection of other rhymes about forms of transport.

Mathematical development
● Use triangles and squares to discover more about tessellating shapes.
● Introduce the concept of paying money and receiving a ticket.

Knowledge and understanding of the world
● Investigate the rotating wheels and the pop-up passengers. Compare them with the books and toys you have in your setting.

Creative development
● Create a role-play bus with a driver, tickets, seats, and clothes.

Encourage those who have been on a bus ride to share their experiences with everybody in your setting.

An Elephant Goes Like This and That

Learning objectives: to create a working display; to gain an increasing command of descriptive vocabulary.

What you need

Black backing paper; silver spray paint (adult use); gold sticky stars; red cord; gold border paper; white, yellow and gold card; gold foil paper; gold glitter glue; large hole punch; white, red and black painting paper; metallic paints; grey paint; brushes; coloured sand and glitter; red map pins; large pieces of strong cardboard; newspapers; PVA glue; wire; coloured beads; two long nails; hammer; the rhyme 'An Elephant Goes Like This and That' from *This Little Puffin...* compiled by Elizabeth Matterson (Puffin Books); pictures of

Indian elephants in festival decoration; information books and story-books about elephants; Indian artefacts; elephant toys.

What to do

Familiarize the children with the rhyme 'An Elephant Goes Like This and That'. Encourage them to swing to the steady rhythm of the rhyme as you recite it together. Consult the information books with the children and invite them to help you make a working display.

Cover the display board with black backing paper and add a gold border. An adult should spray the backing paper with silver spray paint, then add some gold stars. Look at pictures of Indian elephants in festival decoration and choose a two-colour theme based on the pictures – we chose red and yellow. Cut lengths of yellow card and secure them to the board to make a temple floor and pillars. Use a large hole punch

Using the display
Communication, language and literacy
● Make collections of other descriptive opposite words, then invite the children to make up a group poem.

Mathematical development
● Create patterns with beads, peg boards or mosaics.

Knowledge and understanding of the world
● Help the children to use a map, atlas or globe to find out exactly where India is in relation to where they live.
● Investigate the differences between Indian and African elephants.

Physical development
● Play some appropriate music and encourage the children to lumber around like elephants. Can they also move like a tiny animal, such as a mouse? Play a music and movement game where the children have to listen to the change in the music and adjust their movements to suit.

Creative development
● Use musical instruments to perform a steady beat when you are reciting the rhyme together.
● Try to borrow some real Indian instruments for the children to handle.

to make decorative edges for the pillars. On one pillar, mount the complete version of the rhyme. On the other, mount some facts about elephants that the children have found out.

Cut two large domes of yellow card for the tops of the pillars. Rule lines on the domes and invite the children to glue squares of gold foil paper neatly between the lines. Disguise the pencil lines with gold glitter glue. Secure the domes to the tops of the pillars. Use a strip of gold card secured with red map pins to make the temple roof. Cut squares of red and black painting paper, then ask the children to create tiles for the temple floor by pouring coloured sand and glitter over drizzled glue. Suspend some of the tiles back to back above the display.

Cut an elephant's body, head and tail from strong cardboard. Invite the children to cover the three pieces of card with ripped newspaper and a mixture of grey paint and PVA glue. Leave to dry for a day or two.

Cut a blanket and head-dress from red paper. Give the children pre-drawn grids, four squares by four and ask them to use metallic paints to make each square on their grid a different tone. When the squares are dry, stick them onto the blanket and head-dress and use the punched paper discs from the pillars for decoration. Give the elephant tusks and eyes cut from white card.

Invite the children to thread coloured beads onto short pieces of wire. Secure these in bunches, like tassels, to a piece of red cord running along the edge of the elephant's blanket and head-dress and also around its legs.

Secure the elephant's body into the centre of the temple, then use two large nails to hang the head and tail in place. Disguise the nail on the head-dress with another tassel of beads. The head and tail of the elephant should swing freely.

Write or cut out the first line of the rhyme to make a caption. Add other descriptive opposite words down either side of the display. Below the display, arrange a collection of Indian artefacts, elephant toys and story-books.

Talk about
● Find out more about the important role of the Indian elephant.

Home links
● Tell carers about your work on elephants. They might like to arrange a visit to a safari park to see some real elephants.
● If you have an Indian family in your setting, take the opportunity to invite an adult in to talk to the children about life in India.

Come and tell a rhyme

Learning objectives: to encourage performance skills; to encourage character role-play with the use of puppets and toys.

What you need

A puppet theatre or small table; a collection of puppets or toys which link to nursery rhymes; a selection of visual clues for each rhyme; a play microphone.

What to do

Set up a puppet theatre in an open area. Mount some prompt cards to encourage the children to think about which rhyme they would like to perform. Include visual clues such as a picture of a bus, or a soft-toy spider. Place the puppets and toys nearby, then invite the children to use the area to perform rhymes to each other. As they become more confident, you could tape their performances, and then let the children share the tape with their carers at collection time.

Talk about

● Talk about how we can change our voices to give different characters their own personality. This activity can be used during a circle time with no puppets. Decide on a character and let each child who wants to say a short sentence in character.
● Discuss new puppets and toys that you could add to your puppet theatre.

Home links

● Tell carers about the activities that their children are involved in, and encourage them to set up a similar activity at home.
● Suggest that carers consider taking their children to a professional puppet show at the local theatre. Encourage those who have been to talk about their experience.
● Make a list of suitable story tapes for the children in your setting. These will encourage listening skills and also give some carers a well-earned break on busy days!

Further display table ideas

● The children will enjoy making masks of rhyme characters and some will feel more comfortable performing rhymes while wearing their masks. Most toy shops sell masks that will be strong enough for role-play over a few days.
● If the children are not comfortable with using masks or puppets, provide a range of hats to encourage role-play.

STORY AND RHYME

Counting rhymes

Children cannot fail to be inspired and enthused by the stunning designs in this chapter. From little monkeys to speckled frogs, the interactive displays all provide opportunities to develop a wide range of skills across the curriculum.

Frogs

Learning objectives: to develop interest in working with numbers; to practise counting and matching; to gain understanding of ordering.

What you need
Green, yellow, brown and black card; green papers; Velcro; *Apusskidu: Songs for Children* edited by Beatrice Harrop (A & C Black); five frog outlines; glue; two sets of pre-cut numbers from 1 to 5.

What to do
Back a display board with blue paper. Cut a log from black cardboard and attach strips of brown card to represent bark. Glue a pre-cut number on each frog, and attach Velcro to the reverse of each frog. Mount the log on the board. Use the green papers to make grasses for the lower edge of the display. Cut five lily pads from green card and number them from 1 to 5. Attach a corresponding number of flowers, made from green and yellow card, to each lily pad. Attach Velcro to the reverse of the lily pads and mount on the board. Place a series of questions around the edges of the board to stimulate interaction with the display.

Learn the rhyme 'Five Little Speckled Frogs', found in *Apusskidu*. Invite five children to stand at the front of the group and act out the rhyme.

When the children are familiar with the rhyme, introduce the display. Invite them to arrange and rearrange the display using the question prompts around the board.

Talk about
● Discuss the order of the frogs. Arrange them on the log in the correct order.
● Encourage the children to use the display with a friend, taking turns to set each other tasks.

Home links
● Suggest other ways for carers to work on ordering and matching with their children. These include ordering toys by size, matching socks together after washing, matching shoes with the correct colour shoe polish and so on.

Five blue boats

Learning objectives: to use rhymes to discuss sets and quantity; to talk about water safety.

What you need

White and black painting paper; paints; a variety of brushes; pencils; crayons; scissors; cardboard combs; marbling inks; sticks; PVA glue; five margarine tubs; blue fabric scraps; cardboard egg-boxes; five play people; the 'One blue boat' photocopiable sheet on page 79; blue fabric; plastic beads; thread; sand; collection of sailing artefacts; small water tank; plastic boats; the rhyme 'One Blue Boat Sailing on the Sea' from *One Blue Boat* by Linda Hammond (Puffin Books – out of print, try libraries).

What to do

Enjoy the rhyme 'One Blue Boat Sailing on the Sea' with the children, then suggest that they help you to create a display featuring five boats.

Provide strips of paper and invite the children to experiment with different techniques to create grey and blue paintings. When dry, arrange the strips at an angle on the top half of the board to create a stormy sky. Mix grey tones using black and white paint, then invite the children to paint some cardboard egg-boxes. Arrange these at the top of the display to make stormy clouds. In front of the clouds, suspend threaded lines of blue and transparent beads to represent rain.

Provide the children with squares of painting paper and invite them to use other techniques such as marbling, sponging or dragging cardboard combs to make a stormy sea. Cut wavy lines along the long edges of the paintings before mounting.

Ask five children to paint the margarine tubs with a mixture of blue paint, sand and PVA glue. This will help the paint to stick to the plastic. When the boats are dry, staple them to the display on the stormy sea. Add painted

Using the display
Personal, social and emotional development
● In small groups, discuss what it would be like to be on a boat during a storm. Would you be afraid? What would you eat and drink to keep warm? How would you know which way to sail?

Communication, language and literacy
● Think about stormy weather and seas. Make a collection of more descriptive words to add to your display.

Mathematical development
● Think about sets of five. Ask the children to draw five boats and then to add five flags and five captains.
● Fill a water tray and float some margarine tubs. Give the children five marbles or pebbles and let them see how many they can float before their boats sink.

Knowledge and understanding of the world
● Make boats with junk materials or modelling clay. Add sails and see if the boats float. Discuss what makes a boat float or sink.
● Experiment with ways to move a toy boat across the water tray. Try blowing, making waves and so on.

Physical development
● Talk about the sea and about how the weather affects it. Listen to some sea songs and encourage the children to move to the music. *High Low Dolly Pepper* by Veronica Clark (A & C Black) contains some good sea songs.

Creative development
● Role-play the rhyme, and other rhymes and stories about boats.
● Make a boat from large bricks or cardboard boxes and encourage the children to go sailing.

---

sticks for masks, and make sails from blue fabric scraps. Place the masks at a slight angle to look as if they are being blown by the wind.

Add white paper flags to the boats, numbered from 1 to 5, and put a play-person captain in each boat. Use some lines from the rhyme as a title for your display and add suitable words to the stormy sky.

Give each child a copy of the photocopiable sheet on page 79. Ask them to cut out, arrange and glue the hull and sails of their boat onto the stormy background. Let them decorate their boats using their choice of colouring equipment. Display the finished pictures along the bottom of the display.

Arrange a fabric-covered table beneath the display. On this, arrange a collection of sailing artefacts, a small water tank, partially filled with water, and some plastic boats for the children to explore. Remember to add a complete version of the rhyme for carers to read as they explore the display with their children.

Talk about
● Discuss the artefacts at the bottom of the display.
● Talk about enjoying the water safely and learning to swim.
● Talk about sailing clothes. What fabrics are they made from? Discuss why they are made from such brightly-coloured fabrics.

Home links
● Invite any carers who have sailing skills to come in to talk to the children about their experiences.
● Inform carers about what you have been talking about. Suggest that they carry on the discussion about water safety at bath-time, and that they play with toy boats with their children.

Interactive display

Five Little Monkeys

Learning objectives: to encourage awareness of subtraction; to gain understanding of ordering.

What you need
Pale blue and yellow backing paper; white paper; paints; brushes; cardboard combs; white sand; silver glitter; junk boxes; brown parcel paper; stiff brown cardboard; scissors; green card; split-pin fasteners; salt dough; empty plastic screw-lid jar; sticky tape; PVA glue; small toy monkey (or cardboard cut-out) and boat; yellow fabric; collection of five soft toy monkeys; five birthday badges; five T-shirts (numbered from 1 to 5 with permanent dye crayons); five plastic bananas; *The Kingfisher Nursery Collection* (Kingfisher Books – out of print, try libraries).

What to do
Enjoy the rhyme with the children, then suggest that they might like to help to make some little monkeys of their own! Cover the top half of the display board with pale blue paper and the bottom half with yellow paper. Invite the children to paint the sea by covering white paper with thickened blue and green paint and using card combs to make waves. Make the sea look even more inviting by adding white sand and silver glitter for the foam. When the sea is complete, staple it onto the centre of the board.

Use gold paint to stipple some texture onto the yellow paper to represent sand. Add a gold border to the bottom half and a pale blue border to the top half of the display. Cut out paper banana shapes and number them from 1 to 5. Mount these around the border.

Cut strips of brown parcel paper and encourage the children to practise their cutting skills by fringing down one side of each piece. Cover junk boxes with the fringed paper and then arrange the boxes over each other to make the trunk of the banana tree. Cut five leaves for the banana tree from green

card, and let the children decorate these with green and yellow paint handprints. When the leaves are dry, staple them into position at the top of the tree.

Cut heads, faces, bodies, limbs and tails for four monkeys from stiff brown cardboard. Let the children paint each monkey with brown tones, using pinker shades for the face. When dry, add details to the faces. Discuss with the children how to join the monkeys with the split-pin fasteners and where to place them in the tree.

Encourage the children to model some bananas from salt dough. Before baking, insert a paper clip into the top of each one so that they can be hung from the display. When they have been baked, let the children paint the bananas with yellow paint and add brown markings with fine brushes. Seal the paint with a layer of PVA glue. Suspend some of the bananas from the tree, and scatter some on the sand below.

Model a currant bun from salt dough and decorate before adding to the display, together with an empty plastic jar labelled 'glue'. Fix a small boat carrying a toy monkey, or cardboard cut-out, to the sea. Number the monkeys on the display from 1 to 5. Add a final touch by including some lines from the rhyme, a complete version of the text, and five drawings of five monkeys.

On a fabric-covered table below the display, arrange a collection of five soft-toy monkeys, each wearing a birthday number badge, and five plastic bananas. Make five numbered

Using the display

Personal, social and emotional development

● Talk together about what it is like when somebody you love goes away. How do you feel? What can you do to make sure that you remember them?

Communication, language and literacy

● Make a collection of other rhymes which employ similar counting activities, such as 'Ten Green Bottles'.
● Encourage the children to find different rhyming words to make a new version of the same rhyme.

Mathematical development

● Ask five children to match the toy monkeys with the bananas.
● Invite five children to put on the numbered T-shirts. Ask the rest of the group to arrange the children in order to make a number line and then to match the numbered monkeys to the T-shirt wearers.

Physical development

● Read the rhyme line by line and act out the story. Pay attention to exactly how different it would be to walk on four feet and to have a tail.

T-shirts available to encourage the children to role-play the rhyme together.

Talk about

● Count backwards from 5 to 1.
● Discuss what happens when you take one away. Use appropriate vocabulary, such as 'one less'.
● Order numbers from 1 to 5.

Home links

● Tell carers that you are working on the mathematical concept of sets of five and early understanding of subtraction through rhyme. Invite them to make collections of five and continue the activities at home with their children.

Five Little Speckled Frogs

Learning objectives: to develop skills in counting back; to learn about the life cycle of the frog.

What you need

Pale blue and green backing paper and border paper; painting paper; variety of brown and blue papers; green and yellow tissue paper; cling film; foil papers; paints; thin bamboo canes; foam; yellow sticky dots; dolly pegs; pipe-cleaners; transparent thread; corrugated cardboard; white and green card; yellow pom-pom; Mod-Roc (available from Specialist Crafts, tel: 0116-2510405); chicken wire; polyurethane varnish; collection of soft-toy frogs; information and story-books about frogs; the 'Speckled frogs' photocopiable sheet on page 80; *Apusskidu: Songs for Children* edited by Beatrice Harrop (A & C Black).

What to do

Sing together the rhyme 'Five Little Speckled Frogs', and then suggest that the children help you to create a counting display based on the rhyme.

Cover the top half of the board with pale blue paper and the bottom half with green paper, and add similar coloured borders. Cut a large piece of paper to represent a pond and collage it with a selection of blue papers. Mount it in the centre of the display. Run some lengths of cling film over the top of the pond to make it look reflective. Cut some lily pads from green card and mount them on top of the shiny surface. Add one lily flower made from white card petal shapes and a yellow pom-pom.

Surround the pond with stones cut from a variety of brown papers. Invite the children to paint pieces of paper with a mixture of green and yellow paint. Cut these into blades of grass and add them in clumps between the

stones. Make some bulrushes by covering bamboo canes with strips of olive-green tissue paper. Use foam, cut to size and dipped in brown paint, for the heads of the bulrushes.

Paint a large piece of corrugated cardboard with brown tones to make the log. When dry, roll up the cardboard and attach it to the centre of the display.

Ask five children to draw just the bodies and heads of the five frogs. Glue on balls of screwed-up tissue to make 3-D eyes, then use watered-down PVA glue to attach yellow and green tissue to make speckled bodies. Use the same technique to cover concertina strips of paper to make the frogs' arms and legs. Number the frogs from 1 to 5 using yellow sticky dots.

If available, use Mod-Roc and chicken wire to mould 3-D frogs. After painting, add several layers of polyurethane varnish to strengthen the models.

To make the bugs for the frogs to eat, encourage the children to paint some dolly pegs and use pipe-cleaners to make antennae and wings. Let them choose and cut coloured and foil papers to add decorative wings to their bugs. Suspend the bugs over the display using transparent thread. Add a title to your display and a complete version of the rhyme.

Below the display, arrange a collection of toy frogs, a selection of information books, story-books, puzzles and models to encourage an interest in the life cycle of the frog.

Talk about
● Count the numbers on the display forwards and then backwards.
● Discuss the life cycle of other animals, such as chickens or butterflies.

Home links
● If the season is appropriate, suggest that the children visit a local pond or river with an adult to look for frogspawn, tadpoles or frogs.

Using the display
Personal, social and emotional development
● Discuss the natural habitat of frogs. Stress to the children that they should never remove creatures from their natural habitats.

Communication, language and literacy
● Make collections of descriptive words about how real frogs feel, look and move.

Mathematical development
● Encourage the children to order the soft toy collection of frogs by size and then by weight.

Knowledge and understanding of the world
● Find out about frogs that live in other countries. Discuss their habitats, colours and characteristics. How are they different from the ones that live in the UK?

Physical development
● Play *Frogs and Bugs*. Chalk some lily pads onto a hard outdoor surface. Choose five children to be frogs and ask them to each stand on a lily pad. The rest of the children can be bugs, and should 'fly' around the area until you blow a whistle. On this signal, the frogs have to catch just one bug each and take it back to their lily pad. Each captured bug becomes a frog when the game starts again.

Creative development
● Look at examples of aboriginal drawings of frogs and other animals, and discuss the techniques used to make them.
● Invite the children to colour and cut out the frog on the photocopiable sheet on page 80. Fold the limbs into concertinas and attach the outlines to lolly sticks to make puppets.

Five Fat Sausages

Learning objectives: to respond to number rhymes with a range of expressive vocabulary; to encourage rhyme role-play.

What you need

Black backing paper; white painting paper; yellow, red, orange, brown and black paint; range of brushes; glitter and glitter glues; five long balloons; petroleum jelly; newspapers; PVA glue; acetate; black card; long card tube; gold card; star stickers; the rhyme 'Five Fat Sausages' from *Yellow Set: Two Little Eyes and Other Action Rhymes* (Walker Books).

What to do

Sing the rhyme with the children and have a discussion about cooking at home, in the kitchen and on a barbecue. Ask them to think about the sounds and smells of cooking food as well as the tastes! Suggest making a display that captures some of this excitement.

Cover the display board with black backing paper. Over a couple of sessions, allow the children to freely express their thoughts about the flames from the cooking fire. Use bristle and sponge brushes and a mix of red, yellow and orange paints and glitter glues, and invite the children to enjoy free expression to paint their flames. When the children's work is dry, roughly cut around its edges and mount it centrally on the display, leaving some of the edges loose so that they curl a little and add to the licking flame effect.

Cut a large oval from black card to make the frying pan. Cover the bottom of the pan with pieces of clear acetate and sprinkle in some self-adhesive gold stars. Paint a long card tube black and fix it onto the pan to make the handle.

To make the sausages, an adult should inflate five long balloons and coat them with petroleum jelly. Let the children cover the balloons with strips of newspaper attached with PVA glue. You will need about four or five layers of

glued newspaper to make the sausages sturdy enough for the display. Allow each layer to dry before adding the next. When the sausages are dry, let the children paint them using a mixture of brown paint and glue. Leave to dry, then add some black fork markings to make them look realistic and appetizing!

Sprinkle different-sized gold card and self-adhesive stars throughout the display to make it look really explosive! Add a line of the rhyme as the main caption and a full version of the rhyme to the display.

Make a collection of expressive cooking words and mount then onto card. Cut 15cm strips of acetate and use these to fix the words to the board so that they move when they are touched. Cut the numbers from 1 to 5 using chunky sausage shapes and attach them to the display.

If possible, position a kitchen role-play area with frying pans, toy sausages, recipe books, a chef's hat and an apron near to the display. This will give the children the opportunity to role-play the rhyme.

Talk about
● Discuss safety when cooking. Remind the children that they must never touch an oven without an adult's supervision.
● Talk about mealtimes. What are the children's favourite foods? Have they ever had a barbecue, or eaten out?
● Discuss special foods for special occasions such as birthdays.

Home links
● Ask carers to take the children to a local butcher's shop. Some butchers make their own sausages and this is a thrilling experience for young children to witness. (**NB** Be sensitive to individual cultures and beliefs.)

Using the display
Communication, language and literacy
● Have a sausage-tasting session. Make a list of words that the children use to describe the appearance, smell and taste of all the different sausages and add these to the display. (**NB** Check for food allergies and dietary requirements and be sensitive to individual cultures and beliefs. If appropriate, use veggie-sausages.)

Mathematical development
● Taste different sausages, then make a graph of the children's favourites.
● Give the children clay or play dough to make their own frying pans and sausages. This will encourage counting development and manipulative skills.
● Have a competition to see who can make the longest/shortest sausage with play dough.

Knowledge and understanding of the world
● Try to discover why sausages go 'bang!'. Do some experiments with balloons using not only air but water too! (**NB** Exercise caution when using balloons with children.)

Creative development
● Make a collection of musical instruments to accompany the rhyme. Discover the differences between the sounds made by wooden and metal percussion instruments.

Physical development
● Arrange the children into groups of five around large hoops. When you sing the rhyme, the children can squeeze tightly into their hoop, but when the word 'bang!' is shouted, the children can bounce and spring around the room. When the children understand the game, introduce other descriptive movement words such as 'wriggle', 'slide' and 'roll'.

Working with 5

Learning objectives: to work with five and sets of five; to encourage manipulating numbers.

What you need
Blue paper and card; white card; three sets of five coloured boats; small-world houses; blue felt-tipped pen.

What to do
Cut a large, wavy-edged shape from blue paper. Make a harbour wall using a piece of white card, and attach this to the blue paper. Using a blue felt-tipped pen, draw some large waves to one side of the harbour wall and some ripples to the other. Place small houses along the edge of the inner harbour wall.

Make a baseboard for each set of boats. As well as the appropriate caption, include silhouettes of the five boats to facilitate matching and counting activities.

Make questioning activity cards reading 'How many boats are out at sea?', 'How many boats come home for tea?' and 'How many boats are still at sea?'. Place these at the front of the table with accompanying total cards of 5, 10, and 15, and two sets of the numbers 1 to 15 threaded on laces.

Talk about
● Sort the boats for colour and count each set.
● Match the boats to their correct colour baseboards.
● Put one set of boats out to sea and then decide on how many boats should go into the harbour.
● When the group is ready, introduce the next set of five boats. Ask questions about colour and numbers.
● Introduce the questions at the bottom of the display when the children are able to recognize numbers and to link them to their answers.

Home links
● Suggest that carers make sets of five at home, perhaps with spoons and forks, and play similar counting and matching games before mealtimes.

Further display table ideas
● Use toy collections of five to have tea parties. Make place settings for matching and colour activities.
● Make sets of play food, for example, five sausages, five apples, five bananas and five potatoes. Make shopping lists with the children, create a shopping basket baseboard, and invite the children to count the correct items into the basket.

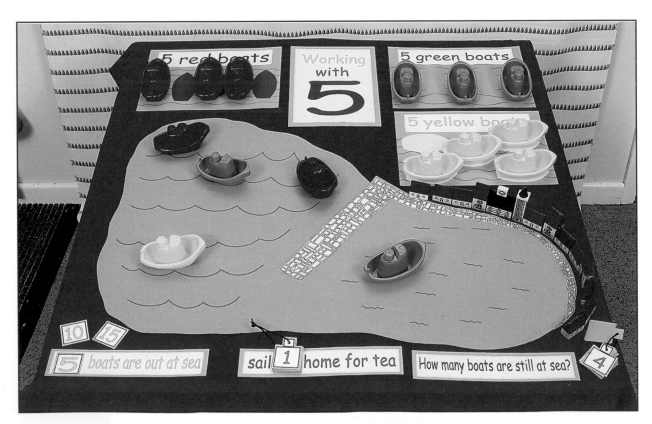

Bird template

Cut out and decorate the outlines to make colourful birds for your display.

Dudley's shirt

Use bright colours to make a patterned shirt for Dudley.

Spinning spirals

Cut along the line to make a spiral, just like Mr McGee's apple peel.

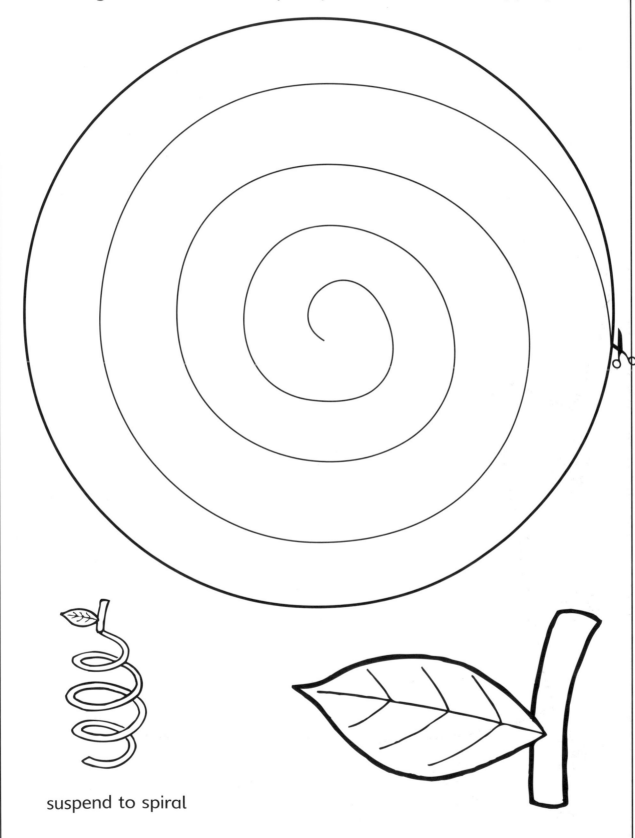

suspend to spiral

Rainy days

Trace over the dotted lines to complete the picture, then use paint or pens to decorate it.

STORY AND RHYME

Twinkle, twinkle, little stars

Use yellow, white and gold paint to create some twinkling stars.

On the wing

Colour and cut out the shapes, then stick them onto painted bodies to make blackbird models.

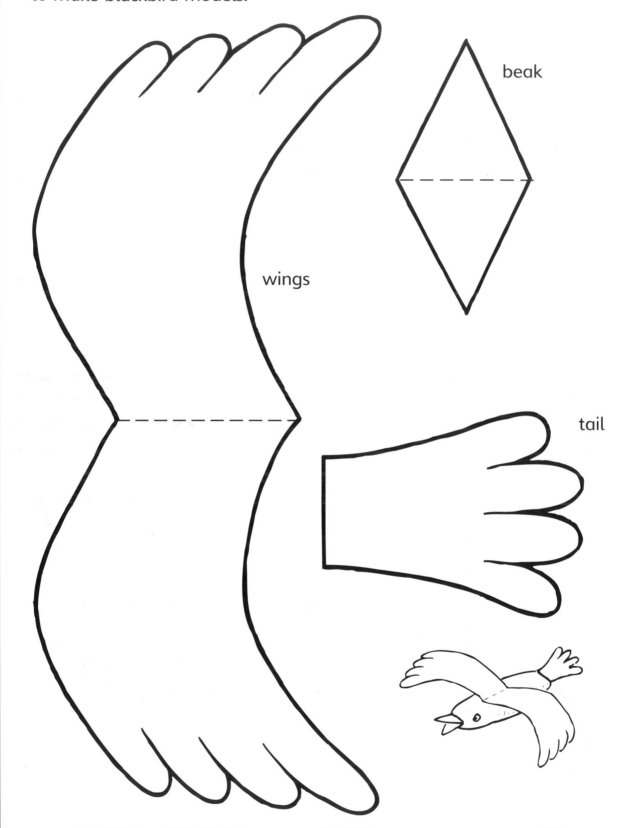

One blue boat

Cut out the pieces and stick them to the scene to create a sailing boat on the sea.

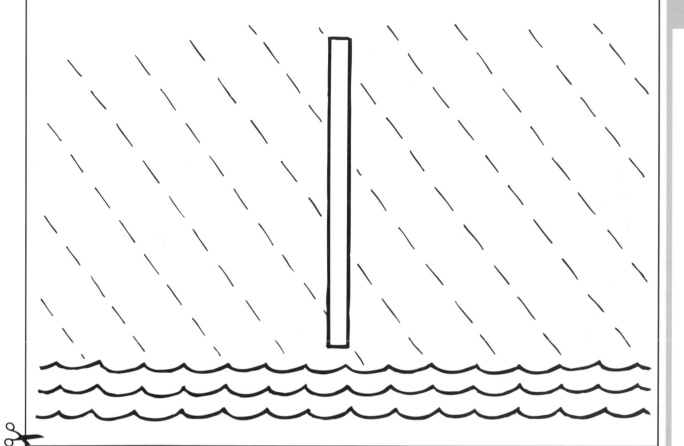

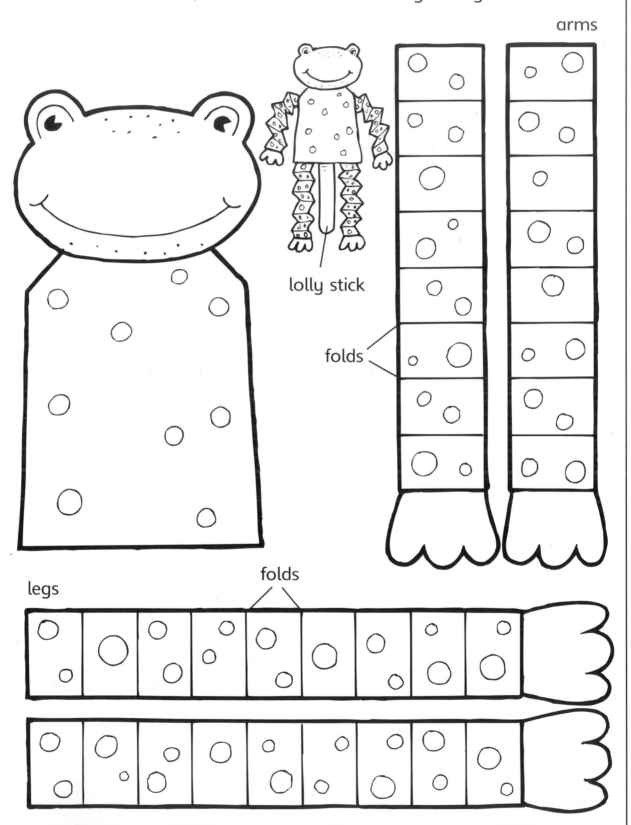

Speckled frogs

Decorate the frog's body, arms and legs. Cut out the arms and legs and concertina them, then stick them to the frog's body.

arms

lolly stick

folds

folds

legs

STORY AND RHYME